For Charlie, and for my Wife Amelia.

Thank you both for the endless support,

The proofreading.

The encouragement.

The suffering my countless trips to test myself.

The tea.

I owe any and all success to you both.

With love,

Luke.

x

5 – 8 Introduction

9 – 16 The Legal Bit

17 – 40 Dartmoor

41 – 58 Tarp Shelters

59 – 84 Fire

85 – 138 South Dartmoor

139 – 152 Campfire Cookery

153 – 186 Wild Food

187 – 216 The Bushcraft Camp

Introduction

'I should not talk so much about myself if there were anybody else whom I knew as well'

Walden, Henry David Thoreau

Proper Preparation Prevents Poor Performance. I cannot recall where I first heard this expression, but it has shaped my experiences throughout my entire life. I am sure that if I had never been taught this simple idea then I would have lived a life far different from that which I have.

Its essence is simple, you will do better if you are prepared properly. Which of course means preparing appropriately.

The level of preparation that is appropriate is different for each person, each situation, and each environment, and does not refer only to equipment. As you will learn over the course of your reading, equipment is only a small part of what it takes to be comfortable in the outdoors. To paraphrase the words of my personal outdoors hero, the great Ray Mears, knowledge weighs nothing and goes with us everywhere.

I have spent the majority of my life outdoors in different capacities. From kayaking along Leicester's river Soar, to sleeping on benches during my homelessness, camping in the woods and hiking through wilderness areas. Over those outdoor years I have collected knowledge and experience. Recently, I was camping with some people I knew from our local pub and noticed how vastly different their skillsets were to my own. Whilst I won't reference that trip in this volume, that experience led me to begin writing this book.

I could have saved myself time and effort by keeping this book entirely factual and simply addressing bushcraft and outdoors topics, but that boring factual style is something I can't stand in other books, so I have included some narrative sections. On my camping, hiking or mountaineering trips, I have always kept detailed notes of the journey; the narratives in this book are almost exactly copied from the notes of three trips I have taken this year.

Now to the book itself, this has been a labour of love for me. I hope you enjoy it, and maybe even learn something new.

The Legal Bit

'His power should every wise man use with discretion; for he will find, when among the bold he comes, that no one alone is bravest.'

Havamal: 64

In the UK we are relatively restricted in our outdoor pursuits by various laws and acts of parliament. I will not speak to their efficacy or voice my opinions in any depth as to the ethics of allowing our freedoms to be suppressed, monitored, or controlled. I intend this chapter to be strictly informative, and hopefully kept mercifully short.

The Offensive Weapons Act

The offensive weapons act was first introduced in 1959 and was intended to restrict the availability of certain classifications of bladed articles. This act has been updated and revised many times, and as we stand in the UK at the time of writing the act has recently been updated again.

This act of parliament affects wild campers in the way that it makes it illegal to carry large knives and axes in public places. Tools that are entirely necessary in remote places. As it stands at the time of writing, a legal knife must have a blade of less than three inches in length, that folds and does not lock in the open position.

There are exceptions however, and as long as a person has a good reason (in the legal sense) for carrying a blade that exceeds this length then they shouldn't be committing a crime. I personally carry fixed blade Mora knives on all expeditions, rarely is the length shorter than three inches and they never fold. As far as I'm concerned, a folding knife or multitool is not much use in the outdoors.

The Right To Roam And Civil Trespass

In the year 2000, the countryside and rights of way act gave the public the right to roam over roughly 8% of England. But unfortunately, land access in England is still an issue and can lead you to committing civil trespass if you happen to wander into certain areas.

Luckily, trespass is a civil offense unless damage to property is happening and is rarely prosecuted.

Wild camping is allowed in very few areas of England, but if you are respectful and leave no trace you shouldn't have an issue. If you are asked to move on by a landowner you should do so, but with carefully selected campsites I have never had this happen to me in all my years outdoors.

It is worth mentioning that if you have a bright orange mountaineering style tent, you might be noticed and asked to move more often than if you are using natural colours.

Campfires

As most people are aware, it is illegal to light a campfire in the open anywhere in England or Wales unless you have the express permission of the landowner. But in Scotland open campfires have been legal since 2004.

Regardless of the law on this topic, it is important that when lighting fires outdoors that you are careful and understand the conditions you are in. campfires are a leading cause of forest fires, and whilst in the UK the risk is low, it is important that we don't have a negative effect on our environment. See the section on fires for advice on how to minimise risk to the environment and for some stealthy methods of fire lighting.

Leave No Trace

This isn't a specific law, act, or piece of legislation, but just good practice. Wildcamping is generally accepted in the UK as it stands, but probably wouldn't be if the people doing the wildcamping were causing a nuisance, leaving a mess, or doing damage to the lands that they camp on. Leaving no trace of your presence is a good way to ensure that our activities aren't looked down upon by the rest of the public. When leaving a campsite, ensure that there is no trace of you ever being there. Remove any and all litter or waste and take it with you, scatter the wet ashes of any campfires and back fill any fire pit that was dug. I even go as far as to ensure that disturbed leaf litter is brushed back over to cover the evidence of repeated footsteps, but that probably isn't necessary.

If everybody follows the simple rule of 'leave no trace' then we are likely to be able to preserve and enjoy the British countryside and our outdoor pursuits for generations to come.

Dartmoor

December 28th 2022 1330hrs – December 29th 2022 1700hrs

'There is no lamb for the lazy wolf, No battles are won from bed.'

Havamal: 58

Entry One

Wednesday 28th December 2022

Day 1 of 3 1800 hrs

I arrived later than expected due to some unforeseen delays in the early morning, so had very little time to hike to my intended camp. My pack was only 19kg when I began but having been out of action for so long it felt much heavier. I definitely need to put some work in before I am back to fighting fit.

I arrived at my intended camp just in time. Within fifteen minutes of lowering my pack I found myself amidst the darkest night I have ever experienced. Whilst used to dark conditions, it reminded me of how truly remote this location is.

Had I not been rushing against the failing light I would have re-evaluated my choice of location. I was too close to the edge of the forest for the trees to provide enough protection from the wind, and close enough to the path that I would not be as invisible as I usually prefer. But it was far too late now that camp was set up and the true darkness had set in. Without the torchlight, I was truly blind.

All attempts at building a small-stick fire in the large mess tin were short lived and ultimately unsuccessful. I could achieve a large fire with ease, but I have no need of a large fire, and it would definitely give away my position. Whilst I am confident that there is nobody close by, in part due to the weather, I still intend for this to be a stealthy trip. And of course, I wish to leave no trace of my passing. Therefore, I have eaten a single ration of nuts and jerky; drank water, two of the four cans of cider, and had quite a healthy ration of the Loch Lomond single malt.

Regardless of conditions, (the wind is bitter and deafening, the sleet is constant and horizontal) camp is healthy, although it took considerable time to set up in winds this strong. Setting up the tarpaulin was a particularly enjoyable challenge.

My hammock is low to the ground, perhaps only eighteen inches high at its' lowest. My tarpaulin is set up close, only about two feet above my hammock, and stretching downward on its long side lower than the seat of my hammock, it protects my back from the wind. This has left little room to sit in comfort while I write, but having the long side facing the direction of the wind it offers much better protection from the elements. The tarp has a small awning on the open side, leaving enough room to protect the small stick fire that I have failed to build, and providing an area where I can sit in relative comfort and protection.

My knives are hung from my ridgeline, accessible and accounted for. My axe rests against my boots on the ground beside me. My pack leans lightly against an ancient stump, slightly raised from the ground by a log to insure against flooding in the event that the volume of rainfall increases.

With all my equipment stored safely and my wet gear slowly drying by my body heat at the bottom of my sleeping bag, I am quite comfortable.

The hike from Fernworthy Reservoir to the spot that I had chosen using Google's satellite view was not difficult, but it held some impressive scenery. I hiked through a spectacular forest covering what must be a huge hill. The incline was often far steeper than I am currently comfortable with, and the entire landscape was crisscrossed with gulley's, brooks and logging tracks so flooded as to have turned into fast flowing streams. I cannot imagine that this landscape is ever truly dry, but we will see when I return in summer.

I happened upon a family of deer during a particularly difficult part of the hike today and did not notice them until I was perhaps only fifty feet away. It is a testament to my camouflage that they did not notice me either. They only came to my attention when one of them let out a loud bark, a lovely sound to hear. With my glasses packed away due to the weather, I could not identify a species. A shame really.

I particularly enjoyed Fernworthy stone circle. I stopped there shortly after 1500hrs for a ration of nuts and jerky and some respite for shoulders no longer used to this kind of exercise. Removing my pack, I wandered the perimeter of the grove that contained the stones and found evidence of a small fire. A previous visitor must have set up a small camp here. They had left a tent peg and a three-metre length of 550 paracord behind. I stored them both in my pack and kicked dirt over the fire scar to conceal it. I also have stored, in a pouch on my belt, a large quantity of old mans beard lichen (Usnea, in the Parmeliaceae family, I read somewhere recently that they can be used medicinally against some gram-positive bacteria like strep and staph. I wish I remembered more from my brief time working in science). I have never seen this lichen growing in the wild before. I have seen it so often in YouTube videos from North American campers that I had made the assumption that it was a specifically North American family. I am glad to be wrong. It has an interesting texture, being of a very wiry consistency. It deserves its common name.

Entry Two

Wednesday 28th December 2022

Day 1 of 3 1930hrs

I was not satisfied with travel rations alone, I have spent considerable stores of energy today, and if I do not replace that energy properly, I will be much weaker tomorrow. A calorie deficit in addition to being so out of practice would not be good.

I tried once more to light a small-stick fire, this time on the ground, hoping that would make things easier. It did not. The wind attacked my small flames more ferociously than before and even with constructing a small windbreak the type of fire that I wanted was impossible. Bringing me to three failed attempts. My ego can't take much more. I have made a mental note to reacquaint myself with the skill of building small fires in high winds.

Instead, I have made a meal of instant noodles, prepared cold. They taste foul when prepared this way and I wouldn't wish to do this too often, but they still feel sustaining enough. It is a shame that there are so few wild edibles at this time of year, or indeed in this environment. A handful of hawthorn or even blackthorn berries would be wonderful.

The wind has gotten much stronger. I can hear nothing over the sound of the trees above me. My hammock swings freely as I lie in it, and it is bitterly cold outside of said hammocks wool lined protections.

I would very much like a cup of tea, but despite the conditions I am incredibly happy. These kinds of conditions are why I came on this trip after all.

I will spend the next hour or so reading and then turn in. I expect to sleep well, and deeply. And to wake up pre-dawn with frost clinging to my beard.

Entry Three

Wednesday 28th December

Day 1 of 3 2330hrs

I have slept fitfully these past few hours. Although I can't think why I have woken now and find myself unable to return to sleep.

I am more than warm enough, even waking once to remove the trousers of my sleepwear. The temperature has not dropped a great deal yet, but I expect a cold dawn.

The wind, however, is incessant. Its forceful rocking of my hammock is reminiscent of the motions of a ship at sea, and is likely the reason for my poor sleeping. Each time there is a particularly forceful gust of wind, the foot end of my hammock catches it and vibrates loudly, reminding me of an old Nokia phone ringing on a firm surface.

I have yet to see any wildlife since the family of deer earlier today, and would be hard pushed even to hear any over the symphonies of the wind in the canopy. I imagine most of the animals, like me, have battened down the hatches for the night in an attempt to escape these inhospitable conditions.

Entry Four

Thursday 29th December

Day 2 of 3 1350 hrs

During the night, I guessed the time to have been around 0400hrs, I began to overheat and woke in a sweat. I assume that this was when the wind first began to die down. I stripped to my underwear, lowered the zip of my sleeping bag to expose my chest to the elements and went back to sleep. I have made a note not to underestimate the quality of my sleeping system in future.

I awoke before dawn, around 0630hrs, to heavy rain. I was gladdened however, that the wind had died down significantly. I opened an energy drink, (terrible I know, but I detest coffee) and rolled myself a cigarette. Waking up slowly, to the sleepy sounds of a winter forest at dawn, is one of my favourite things in life.

Once properly awake I began preparing to leave camp.

I dressed, putting on my outer shell to combat the chill that was sure to come with the rising sun, and began with an equipment check.

Experience had ensured that I was in as good a position as any to venture into the storm that was clearly brewing. My pack had gotten damp, (the air itself was wet with a dense fog) and whilst the soles of my boots were rimed with frost, their innards remained dry, if a little cold.

The only casualty of the weather was the large mess that I had attempted to use as a makeshift firepit last night. I had left it toward the edge of my shelter, perfectly situated to avoid the trapping of smokes, whilst still close enough that I could cook from beneath the awning. I record it as an equipment casualty because a swirling wind in the night had blown it full of rain. I cleaned the mess, along with the mug that I had used for the noodles, in a nearby stream without any real issue. The water was icy cold, but not clean. The heavy rain had washed this stream full of sediment, and a questionable yellow foam. A shame, I would have liked to have found a source of water safe to drink from by now.

Camp came down with no issues. I had used quick release knots for both my hammock and my ridgeline and despite the tightening that is to be expected from bearing my 240lbs for nine hours, they gave me no trouble.

Once camp was disassembled, I fought my way back through the dense pine wood to the logging track that I had used to get here and began hiking upwards toward the higher ground and the open moor.

When I reached the edge of the forest twenty minutes later, I realised how high up I was. It was no wonder that the wind had been so strong. I was at the top of a tor, facing another tor to the West, and a rather wet looking valley to the south. The height I found myself at explained why I had struggled with the incline the day before.

Almost as soon as I broke the cover of the trees, the storm that had been brewing, broke. With force. I was once again being buffeted by strong winds, but this time I was surrounded by pissed off little horses and facing a frontal assault of horizontal hail.

Common sense and experience told me to seek shelter before the non-existent visibility led me to injury, but with blue sky on the horizon and the occasional lonely ray of sunshine breaking the cloud, I hoped that the storm would blow itself out soon.

I was wrong.

After 90 minutes of fighting the elements, I had reached the top of another tor. I had travelled perhaps only two and half miles, and I had travelled too far south. There no longer seemed to be any discernible paths close by and the ground was becoming treacherous. The storm now finally ended and I was greeted by a warm, sunny morning.

Removing my outer shell I shouldered my pack and made the decision to head down into the valley, thinking that I would follow the river South. From my vantage point I could see lots of tributary streams running into what I assumed was the East Dart River, but those streams shouldn't prove too much of a challenge. I decided that the best course of action would be to follow the East Dart, fording the tributaries along the way, and head for a small town called Postbridge. Hopefully from there it would be a simple task to realign myself and circle back toward Fernworthy before dark to seek out a new place to camp for the night.

By halfway down the tor I knew that I had made a mistake. I was in trouble.

Every track I tried to follow was circuitous and flooded. Every brook had burst its banks. Soon, I found myself wading down a horse trail. Pushing on, I eventually found myself with about a quarter of the tors' side left to traverse, but the path in front of me had disappeared. Within ten paces I could no longer see the path I had followed to get here and had no desire to backtrack and reclimb the tor that I had come down. In front of me was treacherous ground, interspersed with boggy areas and clumps of grass, rocks, gorse and floods. Behind me was the undesirable climb to the top of the tor along a trail that had disappeared.

The proverbial rock and hard place.

I chose the rock.

I decided to press on along a sodden game trail barely wide enough for my large boots, hoping to reach what looked at a distance to be a more established path.

Yet another poor decision.

The game trail soon disappeared as the footing became ever more treacherous. Worse, upon reaching the ridge, what had from afar looked like a path, was instead yet another game trail. This one more broken and flooded than the first. Left with little choice but to press on, I eventually found myself on a small, flooded ridge. More akin to a smaller hill growing from the side of the other than a true ridge. The ground ahead looked to be difficult enough to traverse that a broken ankle could be a serious possibility. I was facing the choice again to either attempt the arduous climb to the top of a tor and hopefully some semblance of safe footing, or to stick with my current course and head further down. The way up would be difficult, with rabbit holes, bogs, and other pitfalls, but the last short distance to the valley floor seemed to hold more peril.

I was tired and extremely thirsty, I had been sweating a lot during my hiking, and had almost run out of water. I had been relying on the ability to boil water whilst out here and had maybe only a litre of potable water left. With GPS non-existent so far out, I decided my safest course was to face the immediate risk of hazardous ground, knowing that the East Dart River would run through Postbridge.

Within the first thirty paces I lost my footing on a large boulder and slipped onto my back. I was on the steep side of the tor, and on my left-hand side was a considerable fall. Luckily, I managed to catch myself. I severely jarred my left knee in the process, and I had landed on the stainless-steel camping mug strapped to the outside of my pack. That was now flattened.

I was cursing myself by this point, and it is only the fact that I am recording it from a lovely little pub in Postbridge, dry and warm in a comfortable chair by an open fire, that I can look back and not feel bitterness at my own stupidity. I made poor decision after poor decision all day. It is a marvel that I wasn't more seriously injured.

Severely humbled by my fall, I continued. There was such a short distance left to travel that it should have taken no more than forty minutes, but I was being extremely careful, and was slowed by the ever-increasing pain in my knee. I was approaching the valley floor, very nearly there, when I lost my footing again. This time, I had placed my right foot on what seemed to be solid ground and immediately sunk. I managed to catch myself, using all the strength of my left leg just as the 'solid ground' reached halfway up my right calf. The effort of catching myself hurt, but at least I escaped being eaten by a hill. That would have been embarrassing had there been anyone to witness it.

With care I finally reached the bed of the valley and the river that promised escape, without further incident. Now down to less than half a litre of water and very thirsty, I still hadn't seen any evidence of a spring, or any water that would be safe to boil and drink, and this was no place for a fire. I would have to be in truly dire straits before risking an open fire in an environment so full of grasses, even in these watery conditions.

Approaching the river, I saw that it was metres past its bank. I followed a horse trail again, along the western bank. Eventually, inevitably, all too predictably, the horse path ended. This time in a landslip, and I found myself facing another difficult choice. Climb upwards and around through more, treacherous terrain, or ford the river to reach the clear, stable, better trodden ground on the eastern bank.

It was a glimmer in the sunlight that made the choice for me. On the eastern bank I spotted a piece of litter, what looked to be a sweet wrapper.

This time I made the right choice. I had no desire to take the risk of traversing more broken bogs, and the discarded sweet wrapper seemed to promise a clear path back to civilisation. A small voice in my head reminded me of last night's wind. That the sweet wrapper could have blown here from anywhere, but I ignored it, happy to see a way out. I chose to try and cross the river.

Leaving my pack on a large rock I searched for a shallow place to ford.

I couldn't find a section less than a metre deep due to the floods, and I wasn't prepared to get quite that wet, but I found a place where the river cut thinly though the bank. It was perhaps as thin as eight or nine feet across. I decided I could jump it.

Collecting my now slightly lighter pack, (my guess is that it was now around 17-18kg) I raised it over my left shoulder and gingerly approached the bank. This was a risk.

Knowing that to fail would equal disaster, I threw my pack as a shotput, only barely making it to the eastern bank that was taking on an almost mythical quality in my tired mind.

Now my turn. I had competed in the long jump as a child, but I was now much heavier and in much worse shape. I hoped my jarred knee would not cause me too much of an issue here.

Knowing that falling into this deep, cold, fast flowing river in December, miles from anywhere was not going to be an enjoyable experience. I gave it everything I had. I made it. Just.

Landing ungracefully on the right side of the river, directly beside my now muddy pack. I was wet, and caked in mud up to my knees, but was out of my situation and the risk of injury or disorientation was much lower now.

Once I had confirmed that it was indeed a sweet wrapper that I had seen, and that it was recent, I pocketed the litter and decided I would rest here a while to collect my thoughts. I had not been thinking clearly enough through my entire day so far. I had taken far too many risks and had refused to respect my situation. I'm not as young as I once was, and my body complains at abuses it used to enjoy. I need to slow down, think more clearly, and be more careful.

I ate a ration of nuts and jerky and drank sparingly from my rapidly draining canteen.

After perhaps fifteen minutes of rest, I felt ready to continue. I shouldered my pack and began following the river south-east. I had come much farther west than I should have in my efforts to reach the river. The next hour or so passed without incident, crossing some minor tributaries that came no higher than the top of my assault boots, and I was enjoying myself. The scenery was desolate, but uniquely beautiful. In my efforts to reach this point I had paid far less attention to my surroundings than such a beautiful landscape deserved.

Inevitably I came to another impasse. My luck had no intention of changing for the better it seemed. I came to a clearing on the west bank of the river, surrounded on all sides by steep, gorse covered hills. And I could see no way forward. Though the eastern bank was clear.

Cursing my luck, I dropped my pack once again and searched the area for signs of a path that would lead to civilisation. I must be close now, so I checked my phone. GPS was working again and confirmed that I was no more than three miles from Postbridge, possibly less. I am not sure how long I spent searching for the elusive path that I felt sure must be there somewhere, but it was far longer than I would have liked. Eventually I gave in to the realisation that I would be forced to ford the river again.

It was much wider now, and deeper. With its banks burst, the slimmest place that I would be able to access was almost twelve feet across, and maybe four and a half feet deep at the centre. I decided to find a place where it was wider, but much shallower and attempt a ford. I was close enough to the town now and had already decided to end my trip today, rather than tomorrow as originally planned. I found a place where the river was around 18 feet across, the water was shallower, but fast flowing. I was confident I could cross, but not looking forward to it.

Returning to the clearing, I shouldered my pack and began walking to the wide section of river, when movement from behind me caught my eye. A runner had appeared through a gap in the gorse no wider than six inches. Once again, I cursed myself, and made a mental note to chastise myself profusely when I get home, and ensure I learn from the mistakes that I had made on this trip. I had almost forded the river again. Never in my hundreds of adventures into wild places have I ever made such poor decisions, or so frequently. I need to analyse that.

Tracing the steps of the runner brought me to the top of a small rocky tor, and a clearly defined path. The most clearly defined path that I had seen in the last 24 hours. I beamed. Following this path for a short while brought me in sight of civilisation. I checked my phone and discovered that it had full reception again, so I sent a message to my wife, asking her if she would be able to come to collect me a day early, and that I was heading to a small town called Postbridge. She agreed, and I looked forward to telling her about my experiences, and what I had learned.

That brings us up to date, my wonderfully accommodating wife has just walked through the front door of the comfortable pub in which I have written this, so there is no time to proofread. I think it is time for another pint and a conversation with my wife before the long drive home.

Dartmoor beat me this time. But I will be back. Armed with better information and a clearer state of mind. And a map, that would have saved me a lot of trouble.

Thursday 29th December 2022 1700hrs

Tarp Shelters

'A better burden on the way no man bears than much good sense; that is thought better than riches in a strange place; such is the strategy of the penniless.'

Havamal: 10

There are many different shelter types that people use when camping. Tents being of course the most common. Because tents are so common, and because I almost never use them, they have been omitted from this book in favour of a more comprehensive look at tarp shelters.

In this chapter I will outline some of the basic styles of shelters that people build with tarps. Some of these are suitable for hammock camping, and some of them are better suited for open moors and fields, but all of them have their place in keeping you protected from the elements.

The Basic 'A' Frame

The basic 'A' frame is the king of tarp shelters. Simple and effective, this is the design that I turn to in most conditions. This tarp set-up is best in conditions of low wind, because it won't protect you if there's a strong wind to blow rain beneath it.

A simple truckers hitch will give you the perfect ridgeline. For this type of design, I tend to tie my ridgeline at about shoulder height. This gives me plenty of room to manoeuvre beneath it, and I can tie the hammock a little lower so that I can sit up comfortably.

Place your tarpaulin evenly over the top of your ridgeline. If your tarpaulin has centre eyelets, secure them to the same trees you have tied your ridgeline to so that it doesn't move when tightening your corners.

Once your tarp is in position tying off the corners is simple. Pegs will suffice in most ground conditions, but I usually prefer to tie lines from each corner for extra security in the case of high winds.

Put your hammock up underneath the tarp and you are ready to go.

This style of shelter gives good all-round protection from the elements. With a larger tarpaulin it can be erected higher up to give you a workable living space too, making it great for use on extended trips.

The Wind Shed

This is the type of shelter I used during the disastrous trip to Dartmoor in December that I mentioned earlier. It is perfect for those conditions. When there is a strong wind from one direction this design will keep you dry and sheltered all night, and was arguably the most successful event of that trip.

Using the standard Truckers Hitch method, set up your ridgeline horizontal to the wind direction. Place three quarters of the tarp over the ridgeline and secure it on the side that the wind is coming from. If the angle is too steep your tarp will act as a kite, too shallow and it won't protect you efficiently. You want the wind facing side of the tarp to end below the lowest point of your hammock to shelter you from the wind, or pegged down at ground level if you will be sleeping on the ground.

The remaining quarter of your tarp will act as an awning to protect you and your gear from any rain, or drips from the branches above you.

Reminder – when setting up in high winds, secure your tarp as tight as possible, and use every available eyelet. In my experience, the strongest winds can rip the eyelets from cheaper tarps if they are overburdened. Spread that burden out as much as possible.

The Basic Lean To

This is the simplest form of tarp shelter there is. It doesn't even require a ridgeline necessarily.

This type of shelter isn't necessarily optimised for hammock camping but can become a really useful design to use if you're sleeping directly on the ground. Especially in conditions where a strong wind is blowing from a single direction, such as on the coastline.

This does work better the larger the tarp but is possible with the standard eight by ten, or even smaller.

As with all tarp shelter designs listed so far, look for two trees that are about the right distance apart first. But if no trees are available, two strong uprights can be driven into the ground. I have used old tent poles and even arrows from my longbow for this purpose at need.

Secure two parallel corners of your tarp to those trees or uprights at about waist height. Trail the tarpaulin out in one direction and peg it down. Or, if the ground is wet, trail the tarpaulin back underneath you to provide a ground sheet for sleeping on.

This type of shelter produces a large area beneath it for gear storage, and a sheltered space to sleep.

The Dining Fly

Originally designed for multiple people to eat together outdoors, this shelter is very similar to the Basic A frame that I mentioned earlier but is typically much higher up and done with a larger tarp. It can be used in the open with poles, but due to my proclivity for hammock camping necessitating forest camps, I typically use the trees around me. The most difficult part of the setup is usually finding a space large enough to erect it in woodland.

When using this set up, I typically take a tarp measuring twelve by twelve feet. The large size of the tarp giving me the opportunity to put it much higher, (usually around eight and a half feet at the centre) effectively creating a living area beneath it. Secure each corner of the tarp to a tree, and place a tall pole driven into the ground in the centre to create a domed roof.

I take advantage of this larger space for longer trips where I utilise a base camp. It provides enough space that I can keep a small cooking fire, somewhere to sit on one side of my hammock, and an area to store my equipment on the other. On long trips that extra space to be comfortable can be invaluable.

The Bivouac

This set up is not suitable for hammock camping. But is the ultimate solo camping tarp shelter if you're sleeping on the ground.

I have included this in my list because I have had to rely on it when trees are not available. This usually happens for me on trips where I plan to hike from forest to forest, stopping in the trees at night, when for whatever reason I haven't arrived at the next forest in time. In those scenarios, a bivvy is the way to go.

Using a hiking pole, or sturdy stick as the high point, to rest of your tarp is stretched back into a thin triangle shape and pegged down with tent-pegs or sticks, or perhaps weighed down with stones. If done properly, the tarp folds to provide a ground sheet, keeping out the damp.

Be aware, unless the hiking pole is secured tightly, it can fall in strong winds, collapsing your shelter on top of you. From experience, this is not a nice way to wake up at 3am.

This shelter is not as comfortable as a hammock, especially if you don't have a sleeping mat, but it's better than nothing when needs must.

The A-Frame Bivvy

This shelter is similar to the first shelter I listed. The only difference being that it is set up at ground level. Unsuitable for hammock camping, this shelter is best used in dry conditions with high wind. This design can really help keep you out of the weather and is really simple to set up.

Using hiking poles, branches, or trees, (I have even used my bicycle for one end at times, and usually keep two old tent poles in my bag for this purpose) you set a ridgeline. Place the tarp over the ridgeline and peg it down. Using guy lines to ensure that the uprights you have chosen are not pulled into the centre, you're ready to go.

Whilst all of these designs have merit and are all useful to know. I should admit than in most circumstances I only ever use the basic A frame and the wind shed. Occasionally reverting to the bivouac or lean-to in times of crisis, such as navigational mistakes or kit failure.

There are a lot of camping guides, survival handbooks and online resources that will detail design after design after design, but inevitably, a good all-rounder, efficiently used, will outdo any of the specialist shelter designs in most conditions.

The Stall

As the name suggests, this shelter resembles a market stall. A wall on one side of the shelter can be helpful if camping with a group and you would like some privacy. My wife uses a variation of this shelter occasionally so she will have somewhere to get changed out of the way of the rest of the group.

Starting with the ridgeline as normal, place your tarp over it, with lengths of equal size. One end should be pegged directly into the ground, and the other tied at a right angle to create a flat roof. A very gentle slope is enough to keep water from pooling atop your tarp if the lines are kept very taught.

This shelter design is great in good weather, but I find that it comes up a little short in winter. If there is a likelihood of strong winds or heavy rain, this shelter will not protect you to the same standard as some of the others listed.

Fire

'Fire is needful to him who is come in, and whose knees are frozen; food and raiment a man requires who over the fell has travelled.'

Havamal: 3

The campfire is a fundamental part of the outdoor experience. But as I mentioned in 'The Legal Bit' it is important to ensure you seek permission from the landowner before lighting a fire, or at least make sure you light fires responsibly. Responsible fire-lighting boils down to understanding the local conditions, the wood you're using, and the ground beneath you. In certain soils, fires can burn underground for months before springing up in dry conditions and starting forest fires, and in the height of summer a stray spark from burning the wrong wood in the wrong environment can cause huge blazes in minutes.

In this chapter I will break down some standard wood types and how they burn, different methods of fire construction and talk a little about campfire cooking. It may be worth mentioning that whilst I do not consider myself an expert in fire lighting methods, I am proficient in all of the methods I describe and some more that I will leave out, and I spent time as a young man teaching these skills to children and young adults as part of a forest school.

British wood

All of the woods of Britain burn slightly differently and are all useful for different purposes. Some woods produce a thick smoke that keeps insects away, some burn bright and some burn hot. Here is a list of the some of the woods that you will come across most often in the UK.

Oak

Oak wood when split burns quite bright and for a long time, producing hot coals that are good for cooking on. Putting out an impressive level of heat when burning efficiently, oak wood makes good charcoal. Oak will not burn green, so make sure any wood you use is well seasoned and dry.

Beech

Beech wood burns hottest of all native species and produces extremely good coals for cooking on. I use Beech coals to burn indentations when making bowls and cups outdoors. It doesn't produce much flame however, so if you're using a campfire as a primary light source in your camp then it would be best to use another species in conjunction with beech. Beech burns badly when green.

Pine

There are many variations of pine trees in the UK, with noticeable differences in edibility, availability, and durability. But when it comes to firewood, all true pines burn in similar ways. True pine species contain a resinous sap, packed with a chemical called turpentine that burns fiercely and makes a fantastic tinder for starting your fires. Pine wood burns bright and hot with minimal spitting, and though shorter lived than the previous species, makes a great firewood. Pine wood can be burned green at need, although as with all woods that can burn green, it still burns better when well-seasoned.

Ash

Ash wood is fairly commonplace in the UK and is another great firewood. Ash burns a little cooler than the woods mentioned so far, but it burns bright and for a long time. If left in the round (unsplit) it can spit, but ash will produce relatively good coals for cooking and great flames for grilling.

Birch

Birch bark is a useful resource for fire lighting. If properly prepared it will catch and hold a spark quite easily and burns more slowly than other tinder materials. But the wood itself burns quickly and produces a thick smoke. This quality makes birch useful as firewood in areas with large populations of biting insects, and functions as somewhat of an insect repellent. I tend to burn birch wood in the height of summer when the mosquitoes and midges become a nuisance. This wood doesn't produce good coals however, so it must be tended carefully to avoid the fire dying out. When burned in the round, birch can froth and spit, making it a poor choice during particularly dry conditions.

Campfire Construction

Over the years I have come across numerous different opinions on the best method of constructing and lighting a fire, with varying degrees of merit. Of course, as with most things, there's no truly correct answer, and how you construct your campfire depends on factors such as the type of wood to be burned, the size of your wood and whether it is cut or uncut, the fire lighting equipment you are using, available tinder, weather, and local conditions.

Success at fire lighting is really just a measure of preparedness however, and with a little practice and the right preparations you can guarantee your camps will always have a fire for cooking, for light at night or as a focal point for conversation.

The ultimate key is to ensure that all of your resources are collected before you light your fire. Each one of these construction methods will work equally well with practice, and as always, the jack of all trades is master of none. It is better to learn one method well and stick to it, than it is to half remember many.

Tinder

The word tinder may have taken on a new connotation in the modern age, but in this context, it refers to materials that will catch and hold a spark or small flame that can then be used to light larger materials called kindling. It would be impossible to list every available material used as tinder in the British Isles, but I will list some of the more common natural and man-made tinder materials.

Birch Bark

The bark of the silver birch tree (*Betula Alba*) has a great many different uses, from the manufacture of small boxes and containers all the way up to the construction of birch bark canoes, but the context in which we are interested in this material is in its ability to burn readily.

Birch bark when processed can catch even the dullest of sparks, and the oils present in the bark ensure that it burns well enough to light larger materials.

It is important to be careful when collecting this material, as a living birch tree that has had its inner bark removed is open to infection. The outer bark of this species peels readily and is good for our purposes, but the inner bark is crucial to the tree's defences against fungal, bacterial and insect attack.

When taking birch bark from dead trees or fallen logs, it can often be wet underneath, but the outer bark can still be made useful.

To process the bark for catching sparks, it can be 'fluffed up' with the blade of a sharp knife, once adequately fluffed, the birch bark will catch sparks easily and will readily be blown into flame.

Pine Resin

The resin of the pine tree contains turpentine and makes a fantastic natural firelighter. It won't catch a spark, but when exposed to flame it will burn for some time, more than long enough to light smaller materials and get your fire established.

Pine resin is the living sap of the tree, and rushes to the surface at any place where the tree has been injured, such as in places where a branch has been snapped from the trunk. It builds up over the wound to protect the tree and looks a little like dried mashed potatoes. Collect this material with your knife, collecting it into a container, onto a strip of birch bark or leaf. Personally, I choose birch bark for this process and use the birch bark to provide the flame to light the resin, with my kindling arranged above to start the fire.

This material has a lot of other uses too, such as waterproofing, survival food, and as a thermoplastic glue useable for countless applications, but to describe them all would require an entire chapter of its own.

Cotton wool

Cotton wool and products made from it are an invaluable addition to any tinderbox. I typically carry cotton wool on every trip as it can be easily lit with a ferrocerium rod or a lighter. The 'flint' inside a normal cigarette lighter is actually a very small ferrocerium rod and a lighter that has no gas can still be used to create sparks good enough to light cotton wool.

Spreading out the fibres will expose a larger surface area to catch whatever sparks you are able to produce and as long as your kindling is properly prepared, this material will provide enough of a flame to have a campfire burning in no time at all. I have even used the cotton contained within feminine hygiene products for this purpose at need.

Charcloth

For those of you readers that may never have heard of charcloth, it is an interesting material created for use as a tinder. In the same way that charcoal is produced by burning wood without oxygen, charcloth is produced by sealing squares of cloth in a tin, with a small air hole to let pressure escape, and placing the tin in a fire so that the material inside chars but is not consumed.

This material is fantastic but there are better materials available if using a ferrocerium rod for fire lighting. This material is most useful when lighting fire by friction, or when using an old flint and steel. This is the method that I use it for most often.

I have a camping trip coming up next week, a trip that will hopefully provide the third and final narrative portion of this book. It will be called, 'The Bushcraft Camp' and will be more sedentary than the previous two trips. In preparation for this I attempted to make Charcloth at home so that I could teach my camping companions the skill of using an old flint and steel. In my blacksmithing days I made quite a few of them that I still have lying around somewhere. I've never attempted to make charcloth at home on the stove before but have made it countless times on campfires. I have always assumed that the minor differences in process would produce the same result. As it turns out, a hob doesn't heat things in quite the same way as a campfire, and I should have been more careful in the choosing of my material.

I decided to use a pair of my wife's old denim shorts that she was throwing away. From previous experience I knew that denim made a good charcloth but had to be burned for slightly longer than cotton. What I didn't account for was that these shorts were not true denim and contained a significant percentage of elastics and polyester. When I took the tin from the stove and unsealed it, I found that the material had all but disintegrated as the plastics had melted.

I should have realised really, when the small hole I made in the lid of the tin I was using started spewing a noxious smoke and leaked thick black plastic goo along with the dyes from the cloth. I think that if I am to try this again, I will have to use a more carefully selected material.

Old Man's Beard (Usnea Barbata)

I described collecting this plant for the first time in the chapter titled North Dartmoor. And once dried it provides a fantastic tinder material. I haven't had much experience with it personally, having only come across it last year, but the samples I collected on that trip were dried and experimented with, bringing me to the conclusion that this fungus really is as good as it is purported to be.

It lights readily from spark or flame and provides a good enough flame to light and prepared kindling materials.

Cat's Tail Seed heads

The dried seed heads of greater reedmace produce a fluffy, cotton wool like substance that will catch a spark readily. The fibres will burn more readily if allowed to dry first but can be used straight from the plant at need. If lighting them fresh, they will smoulder more than flame and make a subpar tinder in comparison to the dried seeds, and when using this material it is important to have everything prepared before lighting as the flame it produces is fleeting.

To turn these pond sausages into useable tinder, all that is needed is to pull at the seed heads, exposing the fluffy white core. Be aware though that if lighting a fire in windy conditions this material has a tendency to just blow away given how light it is.

Sock Fluff

As strange as it may sound, the fluff from your socks, or from inside your pockets, can provide a great tinder at need. I have personally used this method more than once when out somewhere remote and my tinderbox has gotten wet in bad conditions.

Particularly with woollen socks, a great deal of fluffy material can be gathered by pinching at the fibres of the sock, the same is true of the inside of pockets of jeans and jogging bottoms. This fluffy material can be gathered and will catch a spark to light your fire.

King Alfred's Cake Fungus (Daldinia Concentrica)

This beautiful fungus is easy to identify and extremely useful for fire lighting. The fungus allegedly gets its name from a famous tale of King Alfred the Great burning cakes whilst hiding from Norsemen.

The fungus is small, dark brown to black and grows on dead ash trees. Inside it is composed of grey concentric circles, giving it it's Latin name.

This fungus can catch a spark but is much easier lit from a small flame such as a cigarette lighter or from another quick burning tinder, and once lit will smoulder. With some encouragement a piece of this fungus can be blown into a large, coal-like ember, which can be dropped into a bundle of grasses to create the basis of your campfire. This is a personal favourite of mine and I collect them wherever I find them in abundance. This was the first fungus I learned to identify, and I fondly recall finding some when wandering the woodlands near to Winyards gap, a favourite pub of my father in my youth.

Thistle Heads

The fluffy seed heads of thistle plants create a tinder in a similar way to Greater Reedmace but take a lot longer to gather. At the risk of becoming repetitive, the process for turning this resource into functional tinder is to gather enough of it, spread out the fibres and ensure it is bone dry before lighting it. The flame this material produces is fleeting, but it smoulders well enough to light small materials.

Of course, there are a great many more materials, both manmade and natural, that can be used as effective tinder. But I think that should be enough to be getting on with and that perhaps we should move on to the next topic, campfire construction.

Kindling

Once your tinder is lit, you'll need to be turning that small flame into a bigger one. This is where your kindling comes in.

Kindling is best gathered and prepared long before you attempt to produce a flame from your tinder and is broadly defined as small twigs or sticks used for lighting fires. When using natural fibres as tinder the flames you can produce will be small, so the kindling you use must also be small. Typically, at this stage I would recommend gathering a good handful of twigs the thickness of pencil led, followed by twice as large an amount of sticks the thickness of a pencil, the same amount again of twigs the thickness of your finger, and finally a good amount of wood the thickness of your wrist or forearm.

Twigs the thickness of pencil led is the best way I have found to explain to people in camp the size of kindling necessary when lighting fires by these means, and I often send my step-daughter toddling off to find some before helping her to light the tinder by ferrocerium rod.

Fire designs

As discussed at the beginning of this chapter, there are many different ways of lighting fires, in this section I will explain the details of a few basic styles.

All of the different construction methods have individual merits and are all useful in different conditions. Platform fires for example, are most useful in snowy or frozen conditions to provide a barrier between your ember base and the moisture in the ground. However, when camping in England I typically use a basic pyramid design in all conditions except extremely high winds, often incorporating a platform to catch embers. I find that this method is the simplest and most reliable, especially if incorporating a minor platform at the base to encourage the formation of a good ember base.

Pyramid designs

The pyramid style design is likely the most common style of campfire built the world over and is simple and efficient.

Pyramid style campfires are categorised by a typically triangular construction. With tinder and kindling in the centre, and fuel stacked in a pyramid shape over and around it.

This type of fire building is quite effective in rainy conditions, but can falter in high winds, and must be fed constantly in its early stages to build up a good ember base.

Platform designs

Platform designs are characterised by exactly that, a platform. Designs that incorporate platforms are best used in wet, snowy, or frozen circumstances to create a barrier between your ember base and the moisture in the ground.

Construction typically starts with a base of large fuel to catch falling embers, such as beech branches the thickness of a forearm, and then a pyramid or box fire being built atop the platform.

A good platform can make any style of fire construction more effective in any conditions.

Dug in designs

Dug-in fire designs such as the Dakota fire hole typically take a lot of work but are invaluable when stealth is a priority. By building your fire below the level of the ground the flames can't be seen from nearly so great a distance. All styles of dug-in fires require an air flow system of some description, most often a secondary hole or channel dug next to the main fire hole.

These types of fires are also quite good for cooking as all of the heat is directed upwards to a single point at which you can hang your cooking pots.

I have only used dug-in fire designs rarely, as I find that the effort taken to produce one far outweighs the benefits, but they do have their place. It is important to ensure that the soil type is not flammable when building this type of fire, however. In peat soils a dug in fire could cause havoc.

South Dartmoor

15th – 17th February 2023

*'I was once young, I was journeying alone,
and lost my way; rich I thought myself when
I met another. Man is the joy of man.'*

Havamal: 47

Saturday 4th February 2023

Planning meeting

Wetherspoons beer garden - Table 104

1500hrs

Will arrived more than a few minutes before me. Telling, because it takes only two and half to walk here from my front door, a good indicator that he is as excited for this trip as I am. Fortunate too, because it meant that I had a pint waiting on the table for me when I arrived, perfect.

I am rarely late. If anything, I am too often obnoxiously early, but the presence of Amelia's visiting relatives this week has left me somewhat confused, my well-established routines in chaos. I am happy that they are here though of course.

Our planning meeting gets off to a cheerfully slow start, passing the time of day and discussing events of the past week. Will and I are good friends after all. I enjoy his company; it can't be all business among friends.

The first order of business is the starting location of our three-day expedition. After some deliberation and copious viewings of the area on google maps satellite view, we eventually settled on Haytor.

We chose this location for a few reasons; ease of access, car parking and terrain being a few. But the main factor in our decision was that this location was known to us already and well known generally. These factors make it easier to navigate back to the right place in the event that we become lost. A useful contingency, as it turns out.

The next order of business is simple.

Transport.

Should we drive to Haytor ourselves in Will's old pick-up truck or should we ask my wife nicely to deliver us?

Easy.

Travelling in Will's truck saves the return journeys in between and saves my wife the driving. Although Will's truck has some mechanical considerations, we are (mostly) confident that it will get us there, and anyway, we agreed that a wilderness breakdown would add an extra element of adventure to the trip.

Now to decide the when. Planning around my stepdaughter means I am only available in those school holidays selected for when she can go to visit her biological father, so it has to be during the February half-term.

Planning around Will's work life means two weeks' notice for holidays. We originally settle for the $14^{th} - 16^{th}$. However, on response from Will's employer we have rescheduled to the $15^{th} - 17^{th}$ of the same month.

Starting our trip on Valentine's Day has earned it the title of being a 'Romantic Getaway', which my wife finds unbearably funny, and despite the date being moved I fear that particular moniker may have already stuck.

Now for the kit list. This section of our meeting took slightly longer, and we were reaching for our fourth round of drinks by the end of it.

Here listed are our individual kit lists as provisionally decided upon. This list will more than likely be pared down to save weight later on.

<u>Luke</u>

British Navy MTP 125L Bergen

British Navy Olive Green 4 Season Sleeping Bag

Cheap Dark Olive Green Tarp 8 x 6 feet

Old Winter Hammock

Mora Companion Knife

Odin's Axe (Handmade hatchet)

4L Water

British Navy Mess Tins

Warrior Compact Stove

Poweradd Power bank 20,000 Mah

Baby Wipes (Biodegradable)

Green Polypropylene Twine

Aluminium Tent Pegs

Will

Green 4 Season Sleeping Bag

90L 95 Pattern British Army Bergen

Cheap Dark Olive Tarp 8 x 6 feet

Standard Green and Black Double Hammock

Mora Clipper Knife

Magnusson Hatchet

4L Water

British Army Mess Tins

JetBoil

Poweradd Power bank 20,000 Mah

Blue Nylon Rope

Water Purification Tablets

Minor Injuries First Aid Kit

This provisional list, I believe, will add up to a greater weight than I am currently capable of carrying comfortably over long distance, especially when considering the added weight of food and the injury sustained to my knee on my last excursion on the moors. So, it is likely that whilst packing we will reduce down the list by removing duplicated equipment. For example, we can share mess tins and stoves, and we only need a single axe if one is necessary at all.

Food is another such subject that received longer discussion.

Will and I are of similar minds regarding food types. We both prefer to carry high calorie food items that can be consumed raw at need.

This ideological similarity resulted in a minor tangent to discuss the veritable merits of British Army MRE rations, and whilst we both rate them highly on the culinary scale of expedition food, we decided on abstaining from their use due to the difficulties in procuring them at short notice.

We did not reach a specialised list or a final decision on this subject during our meeting today and I imagine we will revert to our individual preferences for trekking fare. Namely, the simplest of foods; nuts, jerky, dried fruit, canned fish, ramen noodles, rice, and protein bars. Luckily, despite it being only February and springtime feels a long wait, our combined skillset means wild food is definitely on the menu, and as always is a welcome addition.

There are of course much lighter, more nutritious ways to carry food with us. A lot of wild campers, hikers and outdoor explorers cook meals in batch and produce their own MRE'S of sorts, a fantastic option but not one that we use personally.

Now came the real challenge.

Deciding which whiskey to take with us.

Of course, this is not a necessity, but two young men on the moors in winter are much happier of an evening with a good whiskey to share. This trip also happens to coincide with the anniversary of the death of a very close friend of mine, making an alcoholic tribute a mandatory indulgence.

Our back and forth did not last long.

Will suggested a 21-year aged scotch single malt.

I suggested a 12-year Irish.

Will suggested a 14-year aged scotch.

I suggested a bourbon.

Will suggested a 21-year Irish.

I suggested a 20-year scotch.

We eventually decided to take a bottle each and debate their merits of an evening, damn the extra weight.

Inevitably, being a Saturday and now early evening, our meeting was brought to an abrupt and early ending by the arrival of friends. I would name them, but I refer to them only by their individual nicknames and they are likely not appropriate for print.

The rest of the evening was spent in good conversation with good people. I believe I managed to find my bed at around 0330, much to my wife's disapproval.

South Dartmoor

Wednesday 15th February

Day 1 of 3

0800 hrs

We are almost ready to leave, but still have a few things left to organise this morning. We have all of our kit laid out on the floor of my office and we seem to have everything we need except food and cookery. Both of us had thought we owned camping stoves but neither of us can find them. We add everything into our packs and put them into the flatbed of Will's pick up, but a good breakfast comes first.

After a large full English for me (with an extra six eggs) and an American breakfast for Will we set off for Taunton to buy a camping stove. It is now around 0900.

South Dartmoor

Wednesday 15th February

Day 1 of 3

1130 hrs

We've just been into Go Outdoors for kit, and to the supermarket for extra food. We didn't need a great deal, but it was still an expensive bill. I had forgotten how expensive some of this kit can be.

We brought a couple of MRE style meals each to supplement what we already had, a lightweight camp stove and an Ordinance Survey map of Dartmoor. I learned hard the lessons regarding maps on my last trip, correcting my previous complacency. We are now finalising the kit structure on the back of Will's flatbed in a car park. Our final kit lists are as follows.

Luke

British Navy MTP 125L Bergen

British Navy Olive Green 4 Season Sleeping Bag

Cheap Dark Olive Tarp 8 x 6 feet

Old Winter Hammock

Black Mora Companion Knife

Odin's Axe (Handmade hatchet)

4L Water

British Navy Mess Tins

Vulcan Compact Camping Stove

Poweradd Power bank 20,000 Mah

Four MRE Meals

Chorizo - Extra Spicy

Beans, sweetcorn, Trekking Fare

Five Cans of Cider

Will

British Navy MTP 125L Bergen

Green Vango Four Season Sleeping Bag

British military Basha (Tarp)

Standard Extra Large Hammock

Mora Clipper Knife

Magnusson Hatchet

4L Water

Blue Nylon Rope

Green Polypropylene Twine

Poweradd Power bank 20,000 Mah

Aluminium Tent Pegs

Water Purification Tablets

Minor Injuries First Aid Kit

Four MRE meals

Five Cans of Cider

Snacks and other food

Dalwhinnie Winter's Gold single malt scotch whiskey

By the time we had finished sorting through all of our kit, which was beginning to feel excessive, it was just after 1200 hours. This was much later than we had intended. We had planned to be walking by around this hour. But we still have more than enough time left in the day to get some decent mileage under our boots before nightfall. We plugged in the sat nav and set off.

South Dartmoor

Wednesday 15th February

Day 1 of 3

1500 hrs

We have finally arrived at the carpark just south of Haytor rocks. This journey should only have taken 54 minutes according to the sat nav, but we ran into some minor mechanical and navigational issues which slowed our progress.

The mechanical issue we faced was that the windscreen wipers on Will's truck failed. It had just started to rain at around 1245, and when trying to turn them on nothing happened. We pulled over and it was an easy fix. Navigationally, we were talking too much and singing along to old country songs on the radio, forgetting to pay attention to the sat nav. Missing our turning. Twice. After that we forced ourselves to concentrate. Let's hope our orienteering skills are a little better on the moors.

Now we're here the weather isn't great. It had been warm and sunny when we left Chard this morning, but at Haytor it is overcast, windy and spitting slightly. The plan is to walk to the top of Haytor rocks, find a place in the rocks that is sheltered from the worst of the wind, take out the map and plan a route for the rest of the day. However, as all men seem to do, we turned into children at the sight of a rock formation. Failing to resist the urge to scramble up the rocks, we dropped our packs and started climbing. It didn't take long to realise that this wasn't the best idea, the rocks were slick with the rain and our military boots weren't designed for this terrain. Will offered me his hand to help pull me up a ledge, and we slipped. Falling backwards I landed heavily but was saved from injury by my hair. Having not had a haircut since 2005, I have extremely long dreadlocks, when tied up in a bun they create a sort of helmet on the back of my head. That was lucky. Deciding it was best to retreat from the rocks and get on with the hike we continued on with planning our route.

The route we settled on began by moving northwest to Holwell tor.

We decided to stop here and look for a geocache that I had found with my family on my first visit to Dartmoor. But after half an hour of scrambling over boulders and searching in crevices, along with a short conversation with a lovely woman using a curious sort of off-road Zimmer frame, we had found nothing and decided to move on.

Our path led us down the slope of Holwell tor in the direction of Becka Brook and a lovely little stone bridge. We had made good time so far, but the next leg of our journey was cruel in its increasing elevation. We had discussed hills at length already and thought it best, considering my health and recent knee injury, that when a hill was particularly large or steep, Will would push forward at his own pace and I would take my time, meeting him at the top. He easily outpaced me and reached the top of the half mile long path a good 10 minutes earlier than I did.

At the top we laid down our packs and surveyed our surroundings. Eating protein bars and taking a little water we took stock. With the light beginning to fade, we both knew that we would have to dig in soon.

Choosing to traverse the steep sides of Greator rocks we descended until we discovered the perfect campsite. Will has never used a hammock before, so I assisted him in setting up. However, he learns remarkably quickly and did not need a great deal of help. Finally, in the light of our headtorches, we sat atop our packs, and each opened a well-deserved can of cider.

South Dartmoor

Wednesday 15th February

Day 1 of 3

1930 hrs

Night Nav

So, we decided to try a night navigation exercise for nostalgias sake. It didn't go that well...

For those who may not have heard the term before, a night nav is an exercise used in military training in which you have to navigate with map and compass at night, usually without being spotted by an enemy.

Sitting on our packs with a cider and a mug of the Dalwhinnie single malt that we had decided on together, we were in high spirits. We had not covered a great deal of distance in the few hours we'd been here, but we had enjoyed the exploring, and taking into account the inclining elevation of the last leg of today's hike, we weren't feeling particularly let down by our progress.

Whilst sitting there, talking and laughing, we decided it would be a good idea to go for a quick night nav before supper. Hound tor was only a short distance away and the path was simple. Given that our camp was right behind the landmark of Greator rocks, we felt that we wouldn't even need the map. A decision we would later come to regret. Perhaps the lessons learned in December, weren't learned quite as well is I should have thought.

Headtorches on heads, handheld torches in pockets and camp in order with a beacon light hung from a ridgeline, we set off to ascend the forested slope that would take us back up to Greator rocks. Unladen, the walk was enjoyable. The night sky was clear as we set off, lit up with innumerable stars, but by the time we reached the open moor it had grown overcast. A shame, I would have liked to be able to sit atop Hound tor and count constellations.

The night was much warmer than I had expected, we speculated that it must be around 9 degrees. I was glad to have left my jacket behind at camp.

Before long we came to a medieval settlement that we had seen marked on the map earlier. It was much larger than we'd expected, and we spent around 45 minutes exploring the ruins of buildings and guessing at what they had been before making our way to the peak of Hound tor. Debating at length whether one particular structure had been a grain store, a small dungeon, or a particularly large toilet.

The slope had been gentle, and a light breeze had kept us cool as we ascended. Hound tor was beautiful. Approaching the rock formation however unleashed a litany of references to the computer game Skyrim. From where we were stood, the rock formation looked like the dragon, Parthunax! Skyrim references inevitably led to quoting Monty python and we had a wonderful time wandering around the tor in the dark, laughing and joking. It was then that we noticed our issue. Whilst we were joking around, the clouds had descended. We could no longer see the silhouette of

Greator rocks against the skyline. We blamed the Hagravens.

Both Will and I have enough experience that we were unfazed by the lack of visibility, however. We had both made mental notes of landmarks along our route so should have had no issue getting back to camp.

This experience carried us back to the settlement without any uncertainty, but at that point we realised that during this part of our walk we had been so engaged in conversation that neither of us had been paying proper attention. Faced with a choice of two paths we carefully deliberated before settling on the one we thought most likely, but about half a mile along this path we realised that we were heading the wrong way.

Turning around we backtracked to our last surety, the ruined village, and tried again. I thought to myself that if I had kept myself from becoming panicked on my last foray into the moors and had remembered this simple rule of returning to a known point, then I would not have gotten into so much trouble and may even have prevented the knee injury that was now starting to ache and beginning to impede my walking speed.

Taking the second path brought us to a junction that neither of us remembered seeing on our way up. Assuming we had missed it during our earlier lapse in concentration, we picked the right-hand path and got started. It was the wrong path. We had travelled less than half a mile before we realised though so at least it wasn't too far back to the junction. Once back at the junction we immediately started along the path that appeared to be our last resort. But discovered quickly that this wasn't right either.

Outwardly Will was the perfect image of stoicism, but I'm sure that inside he must have been feeling the same sense of niggling self-doubt that I was. We have both led tumultuous lives, mostly outdoors, and knew we weren't in any real danger, but nevertheless, the feeling of uncertainty when you're lost is unsettling. Especially in a night as dark as this. We decided to backtrack to the medieval settlement again and re-evaluate our position. Without the map and with visibility close to zero it would be foolish to continue walking into uncertainty.

At this point, the batteries in both of our head torches failed, and we were left in almost complete darkness. Luckily, we'd had the foresight to bring the handhelds as back-ups. Sitting on the grass in the dark, conserving the batteries in our handhelds, we discussed our options. Will is a man of action, and advocated for immediately scouting for another path, but I was feeling rather worn out now, and thought we should wait, think, recover, and then act, to hopefully avoid any unnecessary extra activity.

We compromised and skipped the wait, diving straight into thinking. It wasn't long before Will said that we would be kicking ourselves tomorrow morning when we pass this way in daylight and see that the route is simple. I could not disagree with his assessment.

We eventually got up to scout for another path out of the settlement and immediately found the path that we were looking for. It hadn't been hiding, we'd just walked past it in the fog. It took only 25 minutes to get back to camp. We'd been gone for two and half hours and lost for one and a half. It was getting late, and we hadn't eaten since lunchtime.

Taking the spiced chorizo from my pack I sliced and fried it to replace the fats and salts we had lost, adding some goosegrass for minerals, and served it in our camping mugs. Afterward we each nibbled at our individual snack rations as we settled down for the evening.

Conversation had become light-hearted again over another measure of the whiskey and we each prepared to settle into our hammocks. As I was removing my socks, with my boots on the ground beneath me, I remembered that this was Will's first time in a hammock and asked if he needed any help. It is too easy to forget that somebody might be unsure of a new process when they are so competent in other areas. We had been through the basics during set-up, and he seemed to get it instantly then, but I wanted to check. He told me he was fine, and I reminded him to piss before he got in. It's a lot of effort to get up in the night when using hammocks, not least because of the standard unwillingness to leave comfort for the cold and the dark.

Almost the very second he lay back I knew that he was sold. I will not describe the noises he made as the hammock removed the strain from a surely wearied back, lest the moniker of romantic getaway pervade more deeply, but he was audibly enjoying the experience. We carried on talking from our hammocks for a while, until we had each finished our drinks, and we had stopped smoking. Will was in the process of telling me for the fifth time how much he loved the hammock when he drifted off mid-sentence.

Smiling at my weary friend, I rolled another cigarette, lit it, then turned the light off and lay back. Not long after extinguishing that cigarette, whilst looking across at the silhouettes of trees against a cloudy sky, I too fell asleep.

I love Dartmoor.

South Dartmoor

Thursday 16th February

Day 2 of 3 2330 hrs

I am writing this from my hammock whilst Will is finishing his cold MRE. After the last three hours we hadn't the energy to cook and wash up, so we ate our rations cold. I'll get to all this later. We've had a long, busy day with neither the time nor conditions to write very much, so I will start at the beginning of our day.

I woke up at 0845, later than I would have liked but given the late hour that we had gone to bed it wasn't a surprise. I rolled a cigarette and grabbed a drink, deciding to let Will wake up naturally. It didn't take long. At around 0905 he woke up and immediately started reiterating his love for hammocks.

I was glad he was so impressed. He was borrowing my spare double hammock for this trip and I planned to make a gift of it upon our return to civilisation.

We talked a lot this morning, about a lot of things. We talked at length regarding Will's love of hammocks. We talked of how well our individual tarp shelters had held up to the rain that fell at around 0300. Will asked me to describe the plant species around us, their various uses and edibility's, and we had a brief conversation about animal tracking. Before we knew it, the time had disappeared, and it was nearly lunch time. We had wasted a lot of time that could have been spent walking, although time enjoyed can never truly be wasted. We decided to pack up camp quickly and I would cook a modest breakfast of the left-over chorizo with beans.

By the time we had packed, cooked, eaten, and cleaned it was 1155. We managed the climb back to Greator rocks much more quickly in daylight than we had in the darkness and were looking down at the medieval village by 1215. Will had been right, we were kicking ourselves. In the light of day we could see exactly where we'd gone wrong.

We walked steadily for the next five and a half hours, and whilst we didn't lose our way at all, we took a meandering route over some large tors to include places we wanted to explore and covered a reasonable distance. We stopped for a makeshift lunch of Tuna MRE's with sweetcorn on the top of King Tor at around 1445 and spent time exploring the ruins at Grimspound. We reached a place called Bennett's cross with about an hour of sunlight left and decided to rest around a hundred metres from the strange, wonky monument to go over our plan for the evening.

Taking out the map we decided that we would camp in the forest of Soussons down for the night, rather than our original plan of revisiting Fernworthy reservoir. Though I dare say that our decision was heavily influenced by the sight of a pub standing alone on a hill about a mile away. Coupled with the long distance we'd covered today, this sight triggered lots of jokes about mirages.

Once we had decided our nights destination and seen that it was perhaps only a mile's walk on relatively level ground from the pub, we headed onto the tarmac road. The road seemed alien to me after 24 hours on the moor, as if it didn't belong there, but it at least guaranteed that we couldn't get ourselves lost again.

When we reached the pub, called the Warren House Inn, we left our packs leaning against the wall and headed inside. The heat of an open fire hit us immediately and we both became flushed in the face.

There were a few locals inside, but otherwise the Warren House Inn was quiet. We were greeted at the bar by a lovely woman, friendly and amiable. We ordered two pints of Devon red, which quickly joined the list of my favourite ciders, and found our way to a quiet corner table next to a large display case. With my usual insatiable curiosity, I inspected the display before even sitting down. It was full of the history of the Warren House Inn.

According to the display, and to the book I purchased at the bar which details the pubs long history, the fire has not gone out for more than 140 years. An impressive achievement.

Curiosity satiated for now, I sat opposite Will, and spreading out our map on the long table we began discussing plans for tomorrow's hike back to the truck.

The first glasses were empty inside of fifteen minutes, so I headed to the bar and ordered two more pints of Devon red.

Sitting back down I wondered at the time, and not being the type to wear a watch I glanced at a clock on the corner of the bar and was instantly confused. This clock was a curiosity in itself. With the hours encircling it's face backwards and hands counting infinity in reverse. Motioning for Will to have a look, he was as confused by it as I was. This clock became the focal point of quite some humour during our time here and I imagine in the reminiscences of years to come it will likely be a profoundly memorable feature of the already memorable Warren House Inn.

When our time-incited bemusement was over we decided it was time for a smoke.

Having no view of the outside from our corner, the darkness that greeted us on the threshold took us by surprise. Not only had night fallen, but with it had come thick banks of cloud.

Visibility was now down to less than five feet in any direction. It was going to be a challenging hike to end the day.

Heading back inside I asked the barmaid that had been so hospitable, whether these kinds of conditions were common here. I had known that the weather on the moor was unpredictable, but this had certainly surprised me. Our host explained that these conditions, and worse, were extremely common this high up and I recalled that our map listed our elevation at 427m. Estimating at the conversion, I guessed that to give us an elevation of around 1400 feet. She told us with no small amount of pride that this was the highest pub in Devon, and my memory instantly brought to me an image of the licensed café at the top of mount Snowdon, and how much of a lifeline it had been after the long hike up the mountain.

We relaxed again into our seats, with an attitude of confidence. Even if we became lost, our shared experience could be counted on to ensure a comfortable night. We decided it would be nice to eat here whilst we had the opportunity and the menu looked great, even the prices were good, a fact I found surprising given the lack of nearby competition.

I ordered a large beef burger, chips, and salad, with an additional side of chips and cheese, and Will ordered a homemade rabbit pie with root vegetables. Conversation died as the food appeared, it looked great and tasted better. We were both impressed. We finished quickly and ordered a fourth and final round of Devon red, Will bought us each a large treacle flapjack for later and we talked away until 1945, when we thought it a suitable time to begin the final leg of today's journey. We tipped our host, thanked her, and shouldered our packs.

Heading northeast to the path we had outlined as shortest, we turned off and headed into the moor. After a fair distance, now calculated as one and a half miles, we realised that this path was taking us east instead of south. We back tracked almost all the way back to the pub, and saw the path that we should have taken, hidden by the foggy conditions.

This path was very boggy underfoot, with a lot of wet, rocky terrain and we were so focused on footing and visibility that we overshot our turning by about a mile. Back tracking again we discovered where we believed we had gone wrong. The details of the next hour are almost as foggy in my mind as the conditions we were hiking in, but I know that after becoming entirely turned around and walking back and forth for a long while we came to a stream. We sat on our packs and rested our minds as well as our bodies for ten minutes before trying again.

Sitting and smoking in silence, we were supremely surprised to hear a loud whinny less than ten feet away to our right. Looking up we saw a white horse casually chewing some grass and relaxed slightly. Looking at each other in relief we heard the horse take a few steps down the path we had come down. Turning to look at it, it had disappeared into the fog.

Following the horse we retraced our steps, hoping to find a better landmark to place ourselves, when we stumbled across a path that we had missed. Following this path led us to the forest at Soussons down. We attributed this stroke of luck to the white horse that is now and forever referred to as, 'the magic horse'.

The details of our hike through the forest are slim, but eventually we spotted a large area of coniferous woodland open enough for our hammocks and hiked into it. The ground was treacherous, clumps of grasses, tree stumps and gulley's creating the perfect conditions for ankle injuries.

Progressing slowly and carefully we found an adequate spot and set up our hammocks in near silence. It was 2315 and we were both tired.

This location is less than ideal, it is peppered with game trails of various sizes and the ground is too soft for our small aluminium pegs to take hold in. but we managed to create adequate shelters. Both using the basic 'A' frame tarp design, we organised our kit beneath them and breathed a sigh of relief.

It was exactly 2330 when I poured a whiskey for a brother that is no longer with us and said aloud the same words I spoke at his internment and have repeated on this anniversary every year since.

Deyr Fé

Deyja frændr

Deyr Sjalfr it sama

En orðstirr deyr aldegi

Hveim er sér gōðan getr

Deyr Fé

Deyja frændr

Deyr Sjalfr it sama

Ek Veit Ein

At aldrei deyr

Domr um dauðan hvern

As is my tradition I raised my cup to the sky, to our Gods and our dead, and pour it on the ground. Pouring another I toast and drink.

Ritual complete and camp ready, we ate cold MRE's and are now ready for bed. In the time it has taken to write this Will has fallen asleep and my eyelids are becoming rather too heavy to hold up. It's far warmer than it should be in the middle of February, so I have stripped to my underwear and am lying in comfort atop my sleeping bag. Sleep is calling.

South Dartmoor

Friday 17th February

Day 3 Of 3

0800

It is actually 1130 on Saturday 18th but having had no opportunity to write yesterday, I am writing the entire day's events from my home office instead.

I awoke at 0800 and felt great. My body had acclimatised to the strains of hiking and the weight of my pack now. I did wake hungry though and desperate to piss. After dealing with the latter, I lay in my hammock and commenced the morning routines.

Will woke at around 0845 and we relaxed in silence for about fifteen minutes while he woke up fully. For the next half an hour we planned our route back to the truck. It was quite a trek. Both of us had cleared our schedules for the entire weekend just in case we had walked too far and were forced to spend an extra night out, but we hoped to avoid that situation and chose a route that kept us on roads. Given our recent failures at navigation we both thought we should avoid any risk of getting lost again.

The only issue we could find with this plan was that our route would take us through Widecombe in the moor, which having two pubs marked on the map, may prove a significant barrier to our making the truck before nightfall.

We chose to cross that bridge when we came to it and began packing up our camp.

Just as I was untying the twine that had held up my tarpaulin, I noticed an unusual amount of deer sign, and the largest pile of deer droppings I had ever seen, less than six feet from our hammocks. A closer inspection indicated that it was extremely fresh. I estimated that it had been left in the cold hours pre-dawn when we were both asleep. This was a golden opportunity for Will to put his newly discovered tracking skills to the test.

He's a very quick learner and must have been listening intently to my monologues on the tracking skill because he barely missed anything. In the brief time we were investigating, Will had come to the same conclusions as I had, from the same signs. By the size and depth of a rear foot track, the size and consistency of the droppings and by the width of the trail it had left by, Will estimated that we had been visited in the night by a large, adult male red deer. I was impressed with how quickly he'd developed the skills. Talking about the deer as we finished packing up, I opined as to the placidity of deer dispelling any myths as to their capacity to be dangerous. The periods of rutting excluded of course.

Time was moving on and we had a lot of ground to cover today. It was 0945 when we finally left the forested section and reached the path that would take us home, and we followed it due south. Over the next few leisurely miles Will and I spotted more and more deer sign. Tracks in soft ground, scat, and antler rub. I would love to revisit this area in summer when the youngsters would be roaming.

We ate breakfast on the wing. The large treacle flapjacks that Will had bought for us at the Warren House Inn last night. At the risk of sounding hyperbolic, it was one of the best breakfasts I had ever eaten. I remarked to Will that I would be happy to hike all the way back to that pub from my home in Chard, fifty miles away, just to buy another.

Eventually we met our road. The road that would take us south until we turned northeast to Widecombe in the moor. The weather was still unusually warm for February, and I had removed my shirt to avoid overheating. This seemed to surprise and confuse a group of walkers we met on the road at Windtor, but I was much more comfortable without it.

After some steep inclines and an extraordinarily steep decline from Windtor, we finally approached Widecombe in the moor. Noticing a bench in a roadside community garden, we decided to rest a while, rehydrate, and make ourselves presentable before approaching the town proper.

Feeling much better, we pressed on and thought to perhaps find somewhere to eat lunch whilst we had the opportunity.

We made that stop at the first pub we came to, the name of which escapes me. Expecting a small country pub, we left our packs outside and headed in. We had been mistaken. This was no cramped free house, but rather a large, expensively furnished pub-restaurant. We were greeted at the threshold to the main dining room by a smartly dressed male host that seemed to appraise us before he spoke and were shown to a high table against the wall near the toilets. A large table to our right sat atop an unusually large, tanned cow hide. Two northern lads from council estates, thick with the grimes and smells of the moor and wearing boots no longer clean; we felt rather out of place.

A young blonde waitress approached our table with a smile and took our order. Two pints of thatcher's gold and no food yet. Will was visiting the facilities when she returned and I confused the waitress with questions regarding how I should pay, I'm not used to table service.

We stayed for another drink before deciding to reconnoitre the other pub marked on our map, hoping it would be a better fit for us. When we arrived, we discovered that the other pub was closed, and at the bottom of a steep hill that we now had to reascend. Heading back to the upmarket gastropub we decided we should eat here. Will ordered us two pints each whilst we looked at the menu. Whilst we were looking, we were approached by an older gentleman. He had seen us on Windtor and felt the need to ask if I had been walking shirtless in the February winds for a bet.

The menu looked good but wasn't for us. So, we decided to skip lunch, drink up and cover the last few miles back to Haytor rocks, and Will's truck that was waiting for us there.

It was perhaps 1630 when we rounded a bend and left Widecombe in the moor behind us. We estimated that we had about three miles left to cover, so we should be back at the truck before dark, but the hills took their toll on our timings. The incline at Saddle Tor especially slowed us down. Luckily we had chosen a route that we could easily follow in the dark as the light had faded during our ascent. I turned on the bicycle light on the back of my pack to alert any passing cars to our presence and we pressed on. It was almost 1900 when we got back to the truck, and we dropped our packs gratefully onto its flatbed.

The drive back to chard was mostly uneventful, including only two navigational mistakes and a pitstop. But we encountered another mechanical issue when the windscreen wipers again failed to operate. Fortunately, Will managed to solve our issue in his typical redneck style, and we made it back home just short of 2100. My wife was very happy to see us, although she insisted that we both shower immediately.

Will discussed the trip with my wife as I showered, and I did some kit admin whilst he did. Once we were both clean and wearing fresh clothes, we implemented the final stage of our trip and crossed the road from my house to eat too much food at our local pub.

When we eventually returned, (perhaps staying for a little more than just food) we were both quick to bed.

We had both thoroughly enjoyed ourselves, and the miles covered ensured that we had no troubles falling asleep.

Campfire Cookery

'Cattle know when to go home and then from grazing cease; but a foolish man never knows the measure of his own stomach.'

Havamal: 21

Cooking on an open fire is very different to cooking on your stovetop at home, but the same results can be achieved with an understanding of how your fire functions. In this chapter I will be listing five of my favourite simple camping recipes.

It shouldn't need saying that the majority of the ingredients listed in these recipes can't be found wild in the UK, so they will need to be carried with you. In that regard it is best to ensure you measure out any ingredients at home rather than taking whole packages of things. I don't worry about weight as much as many do, but I would still rather avoid carrying an entire bag of potatoes when I only need four or five. Regarding the wild ingredients that are listed in the recipes, most of the recipes can be made without them, but they add a certain sense of adventure to your campfire cooking, and a chance to experience the flavours of the woods. It is worth reiterating once again that if you are going to include wild foods in your campfire cookery that you should always ensure a positive identification and never eat any species that you aren't sure of.

Finally, I won't list exact weights for any of these recipes. Even if I wanted to, I couldn't give exact quantities. I have never carried kitchen scales on a camping trip, so have never measured anything except by eye.

Springtime soup

This is less of a recipe and more of a meal type. Often when camping in springtime, I produce a soup made almost entirely of wild greens, perhaps with the addition of a few potatoes and a stock cube or two.

I found that this recipe was a great way to practice foraging, and to discover more about the species I collect. It was whilst making this soup one year that I discovered that I'm really not partial to the older growth cleavers. I find their stems too woody and their flavour too strong.

Collecting any wild greens that you can positively identify, remove any woody stems. Finely chop three quarters of each species and add to a pot of boiling water. Boil rigorously until the plants have mostly broken down.

Add a stock cube or two, and some diced potatoes. Bring down to a gentle simmer. When the potatoes are halfway cooked, add the rest of your springtime greens and simmer until soft.

I find that wild garlic is one of the best possible wild foods to add into a soup, lending that delicate garlic flavour to whatever you have collected.

Dandelion and Chorizo sandwiches

Fry sliced chorizo or salami in a pan over the fire, add some mushrooms if you have them, and a generous amount of dandelion and wild garlic leaves if the season is right. Spoon the mixture between French bread for a hearty lunch, full of fats, protein, and vitamins.

I have mentioned this more than once in the chapter on wild foods because the morale boosting effect of this recipe cannot be overstated.

Springtime salad

Salads are an extremely varied food group, but in this context, I mean specifically a collection of leaves to be served as a side. In the UK there are hundreds of different species that can be used in salads like this, but my favourite springtime salad consists of five, easily identified species.

A generous amount of Dandelion (Taraxacum Officinale) and Primrose leaves (Primula Vulgaris) form a base for our salad similar to spinach and lettuce respectively, with a delicate flavour. The leaves of Garlic Mustard, (Alliaria Petiolata) add a peppery garlic flavour. I typically use quite a few of the leaves of this species, and a few flowers if they are in bloom. The tender tips from Cleavers (Gallium Aparine) form an extra level of complexity, and the delicate flowers of the Daisy (Bellis Perennis) add an aesthetically pleasing finish alongside their own, delicate flavour. If I have it with me, I'll use a French salad dressing or vinegarette to top the whole thing off. In the heat of a late spring afternoon, this salad becomes a great side for any meal.

Campfire Borscht

Ukrainian Borscht is a staple in my household, and a camp-out favourite. When cooking for a large group outdoors this Beetroot soup always goes down well. Sustaining and hearty, this recipe is extremely simple and infinitely variable. These are the ingredients I use.

Potatoes, leeks, celery, onions, carrots, cabbage, beetroot, stewing beef, beef stock, salt, pepper, chilli powder, garlic cloves.

Begin by boiling the stewing steak for a while to soften it. Add beef stock and garlic cloves. I typically use two or three cubes for a family size batch. Peel, chop and add all of the veg, adding the beetroot last. Add your spices to taste. Simmer until the veg has softened and serve.

Eating bright red Borscht from camping mugs around a campfire is a sure-fire way to keep everyone happy on a cold evening. And of course, many wild foods can be added, wild garlic, wild mushrooms and dandelion leaves have all gone down well for me in the past.

Nettle soup

This is likely the most simple recipe in the list, and has only the one ingredient. Although of course you could add a multitude of other ingredients to improve the recipe, using nettles alone is adequate. This was the first wild food that I ever tried, on an overnight hiking trip when I was very young, and despite the smell, has quite a reasonable taste.

Gathering a large number of nettles, boil them in water until they have almost broken down to nothing, adding more water periodically to avoid boiling dry. Once your nettles are boiled almost to nothing and your soup has a thick consistency and a dark green colour, add fresh nettles and simmer until they are wilted and soft.

This goes well with crusty bread, and although the smell can be off-putting, and the distinctive taste probably isn't for everyone, this recipe is high in vitamins and minerals and has significant health boosting effects.

Teas

There are many plants in the UK that can be made into palatable teas, some of which have demonstrable health benefits. The process for each is the same so I won't describe each in detail to avoid repetition, so here are some of the more common plant species that can be made into teas. The tea making process is simple and doesn't necessarily require any equipment, personally I use a wire mesh tea strainer to avoid drinking pine needles and would recommend that anybody who plans on making wild teas often should invest in one. Simply steeping the plant in hot water for a few minutes is enough for all of these recipes.

Pine needle tea is likely the most well known in the outdoor community, and arguably one of the best. This tea has a strong citrus smell and a very subtle taste that almost defies description. All I can say about the flavours is that they remind me of peaceful spring evenings in the pine forests of the north.

Nettle tea is another contender for the spot of most well-known. However, despite its popularity through the ages, particularly in difficult times, it seems to be losing its appeal. I can understand why, this tea smells quite bad in my opinion, but tastes very earthy and is full of vitamins that can help keep you healthy when out for long stretches during the seasons in which plant foods are scarce.

Elderflower tea is less well known than the others, and understandably has quite a strong floral smell and flavour. This is a personal favourite of mine, but it is worth noting that whilst the flowers and fruit of this species are perfectly safe and edible, the wood, leaves, and inner pith of this species contain dangerous toxins.

Wild Food

With Illustrations by Holly Jackson

'Moderately wise should each one be, but never over-wise: of those men the lives are fairest, who know much well.'

Havamal: 54

The penultimate chapter of this book is dedicated to edible wild plants found in the UK. Holly Jackson has artistically illustrated each species, as I have no skill in that area. It is worth noting that although we have the same name, we have zero relation to each other. Indeed, Holly had been chosen to illustrate this chapter well before I knew her last name.

The UK has a wide variety of different species that we can use for food, and I have listed a few of my favourites, where to find them, and what to do with them whilst out in the field. All of these plants have many uses in the kitchen and in the medicine cabinet too, but I've decided to focus on what can be done with them whilst in camp.

Of course, when foraging any wild food, you must be careful to ensure a 100% positive identification. There are not very many toxic plants in the UK, but you wouldn't want to ruin a trip by accidentally eating of that minority.

You may notice that this short list is devoid of fungi. That is because although I forage and use wild mushrooms myself, there are some extremely dangerous lookalike species in the UK, and I am not knowledgeable enough on the subject to feel comfortable writing about it. Anybody looking to get into mushroom foraging should be looking to buy a comprehensive field guide. I would highly recommend the book, *Mushrooms and other fungi of Great Britain and Europe by Roger Phillips* to anybody with an interest in this area.

Similarly, anyone with an interest in the world of wild food has plenty of material available. This list is only short and as I stated, intended only to list a few of my personal favourites. I would recommend a few different volumes on this subject, namely, *Wild Food by Ray Mears and Gordan Hellman, Wild Food, a complete guide for foragers by Roger Phillips and Food for Free by Richard Mabey.*

Hawthorn

Crataegus Monogyna

Hawthorn reaches a height of around twenty five to thirty feet in maturity, with a spread that covers a similar distance. The branches are covered with large spiny thorns. The berries are bright red in colour, with a large star-shaped pit at the base and the leaves are flame shaped and dark green in colour.

A personal favourite, hawthorn is a thorny tree that makes up hedgerows all over the country. The leaves typically come out early to mid-spring, depending on local conditions, and the berries appear early to mid-autumn.

The leaves of the hawthorn taste like green apple peel and can be a great addition to a woodland salad. Personally, I tend to eat them on their own whilst walking long distances to keep myself occupied.

The berries are much more substantial and can be gathered in large numbers very quickly in late summer. They are dark red in colour and contain a large stone. There are lots of things you can do with these berries, including a form of fruit jerky, some people even refine them into a liqueur. I prefer to eat them raw on the trail as a quick snack, creamy and fruity, they make a great pick-me-up on rainy hikes.

Once at camp, with the benefit of a fire and a cooking pot, they can be refined down to a preserve of sorts. Of course, out in the field you won't be carrying enough sugar to make a true jam, but boiling down hawthorn berries produces something similar that's great on campfire toast at breakfast.

Blackthorn

Prunus Spinosa

Blackthorn reaches a height of around twenty to twenty-five feet, with a spread of around twelve. The branches are thorny and blackish purple in colour. The leaves are dark green in colour and ovate. The fruit is a blueish-purple colour with a small pit at the base. The thorns can cause septic wounds when they penetrate the skin.

A common plant in UK hedgerows, most people know blackthorn as sloe, famous for the gin it often flavours. Flowering between March to June its fruit will ripen in late autumn.

Raw, the berries are incredibly astringent due to the concentration of tannins and cause a strange sensation in the mouth because of this. I am personally quite partial to one or two of these raw due to this astringency, but they are definitely better once processed.

There are many ways to use this fruit, in the kitchen and around the campfire, but my favourite is to reduce them down to a preserve that can be spread onto breads. Once processed this way (with a little added sugar from the brew-kit) they have an uplifting effect and are great for morale when that preserve is made to go with toast for breakfast.

<u>Pine</u>

Pinus

The needle groupings and heights of pine species vary, but Scots pine being a common species in the UK has led me to use that as the basic model for characteristics. Although I have only listed the family name in the nomenclature atop the image so as to include that whole family of species.

Pine trees can reach heights of up to thirty-six metres, with the majority of the branches close to the top. The needles form in clusters, with Scots pine needles forming in pairs. The needles are typically dark green in colour.

Most people can recognise a pine tree, but few people know that those needles are edible. Evergreen and easy to identify, this wild food can be utilised year-round.

The best use for these, in my opinion, is as a tea. I rarely take tea with me on camping trips any longer, confident that I will find a pine tree to gather needles from. All species of pine can be used for this purpose, hence the nomenclature above stating only the family. But some similar looking species can be toxic, so as always, ensure a positive identification.

Pick the needles fresh, and steep them in hot water. The tea has a strong citrus smell and is full of vitamin C. A lovely way to wake up in the woods.

The needles are also edible on their own, but they are woody and have a tendency to stick in the teeth. I have turned to them in the depths of winter in need, but don't recommend it.

Nettle

Urtica Dioica

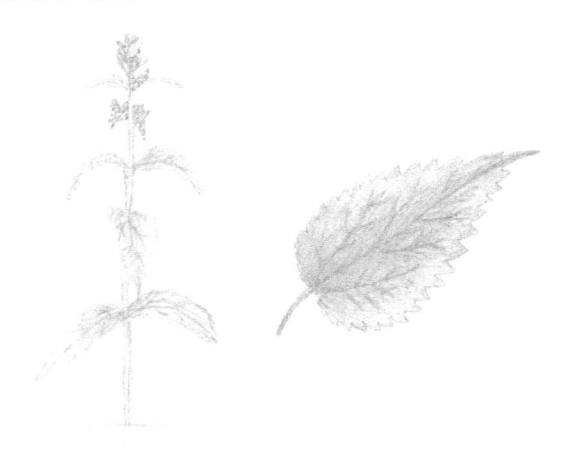

The stinging nettle grows from three to seven feet in summer, and often in large patches. This species is characterised by its pointed leaves and painful sting.

Children the world over recognise the stinging nettle for its painful sting. But it can also be used as food and is often utilised as food and medicine in northern Europe.

Nettles can be made into a tea, a soup, fried like spinach or just wilted over the fire. I'm not personally partial to nettle tea and find that wilting the nettles in the flames of a fire to remove the sting produces the best flavour. However, if you're looking to create a particularly wild stew whilst camping, the common nettle is an easily identified ingredient that will add nutrients and an earthy flavour to your broth.

Another way I use the leaves of the nettle is as part of a sandwich filler. I almost always carry chorizo on expeditions. Slicing and frying it and adding nettle and dandelion leaves makes a hearty lunch when paired with a crusty bread.

An interesting side note about this species is its medicinal properties. Nettle stings can be used as an anti-inflammatory on swollen areas of the body. This process involves repeatedly stinging the affected area and is called Urtication.

Nettle tea is also reported to help break down the acids that cause gout and reduce inflammation in injured or damaged joints.

Sweet Chestnut

Castanea Sativa

Sweet chestnut trees typically grow to a very large height and spread out to almost thirty feet. The bark is typically quite smooth, and the branches grow long. The leaves of this tree are long and lobed, looking similar in shape to the flame from a cigarette lighter, with small teeth along the edges.

Up and down the country chestnuts are used in various ways at Christmas time. My paternal uncle always insists on chestnuts being present at the Christmas dinner table and there are rarely any left over.

On the trail however, chestnuts can be difficult to come by, unless hiking and camping in broadleaf woodland at the exact right time of year. If that perfect storm happens to be your circumstance, roasted chestnuts are a hearty wild food to cheer up any winter camp, with a high concentration of fats and proteins too, making them a great food to carry when hiking.

Hazel

Corylus Avellana

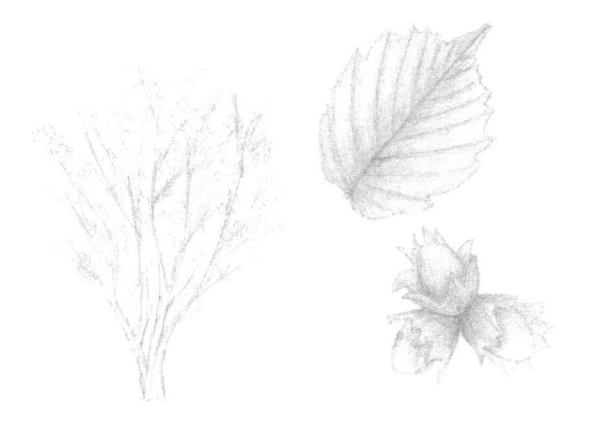

Hazel trees grow most often in coppice form in the UK, reaching heights up to 30 feet and being comprised of many boles. The leaves are small, oval and a pale-ish green in colour.

I would like to think that most people in the UK recognise hazel, or at least it's nuts. They're popular at Christmas time, roasted, and are used in confectionary the world over. To the outdoorsman though, they take on a different class, being high in calories, easy to collect and tasting fantastic.

Hazelnuts are quick to collect and ripen between September and October depending on local weather conditions.

My favourite way to cook hazel is perhaps the simplest, taking the ripe nuts I have collected I place them on the blade of my camping shovel and roast them on the embers of a small fire. This is a scene that I have seen repeated with both chestnuts and Hazelnuts year on year in small country pubs across the rural south-west in wintertime.

Blackberry

Rubus Fruticosus

The blackberry bramble is a creeping vine and typically grows along the ground. The stems of the vine are covered in large thorns which persist and harden on the dead branches. The leaves are grouped in threes and have small spiky thorns on the underside.

The thorny vines of this plant are the bane of trousers everywhere. You would be hard pushed to find anyone that spends time outdoors that has never experienced the bite of tangling bramble shoots around their ankles.

These berries are a staple of the English countryside and are great raw, baked into crumbles, refined into jams, or brewed into gins and wines.

Fruiting between august and September the berries should be a deep purple-black when picked and can be found almost anywhere.

Dandelion

Taraxacum officinale

Dandelion plants don't grow particularly large and are most easily characterised by the bright yellow flower, being made of many petals, and the long, lance shaped leaves that protrude directly from the ground.

Almost everyone recognises a dandelion. Growing up, children in my town referred to them as wet-the-beds. Indeed, the French name for the flower, Pissenlit, means just that. Dandelions are a powerful diuretic, but a fantastic wild food. I routinely pick them during summer walks for use at camp and at home. Even going so far as to cultivate them in an area of my home garden.

Dandelions flower between May and October, and every part of the plant is edible in one way or another.

The leaves make a fantastic replacement for spinach, and my favourite way to eat them is to fry them with wild mushrooms, nettles, and chorizo to be used as a sandwich filler, a recipe I mentioned earlier.

The flowers are a delicate addition to salads and in the kitchen are used in infusions and flavourings for other concoctions.

The stems are very bitter, and I prefer not to eat them, but if your palate is tolerant of that bitterness they can be added to salads and stews.

Even the root has purpose and can be roasted and ground to make a (caffeine-free) coffee. I have not tried this personally, as I don't drink coffee of any kind, but I am told it's a great replacement when those instant travel-sachets run out.

Cleavers

Galium Aparine

This species grows up to two feet in height, and spreads across the ground in large clusters.

This is a personal favourite when travelling with new people. I find that children especially become easily fascinated by this plant given its sticky properties. Indeed, some colloquial names for this species are sticky-weed, sticky-willy, claggy-Meggie's and sweethearts. Sticking it to each other's backs when not looking is a simple way to keep children, and particularly childish adults, entertained on long walks.

Culinarily this plant is versatile, the tender tips of new growth fried in butter with garlic is my favourite way to cook it but it's just as good raw and in salads or added to soups and stews. It even has a history of being prepared as a tea to help treat Urinary Tract Infections.

Appearing in very early spring and flowering May to August, this green is available for a significant portion of the year.

Gorse

Ulex Europaeus

Gorse can grow to an ultimate height of around six feet, and typically forms large, dense bushes. The leaves are small and sharp, with the flowers being bright yellow in colour, small, and being comprised of two petals.

Gorse flowers anywhere from January to June with its peak flowering time between April and May. The only part of this species that is edible are the flowers and flowering buds, but they have a delicate flavour and being readily available in so many places and at times of year when there is little else available in the way of plant food, it can be seen as a valuable resource. I typically use this flower in salads or eaten straight from the plant whilst hiking. In wild places such as Dartmoor this species grows readily and provides a welcome addition to travel rations.

Lime

Tilia Europaea

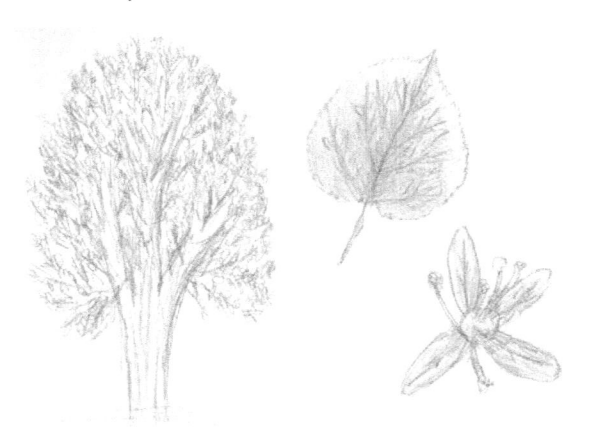

No, not the fruit. I am of course referring to the Linden tree, known more commonly as Lime in the UK. The Lime, or Linden tree can grow to heights of sixty to eighty feet, and spreads to a width of thirty to forty feet. The bark is smooth and greyish, with the leaves being mostly round and pointed at the tip. Historically the bark of this tree was likely used by our ancestors as cladding for rooves and the bole hollowed out for dugout canoes.

The native Lime tree is a tall species typically producing a long straight bole with smooth-ish, pale bark. The leaves are thin, pale green and a beautiful addition to woodland salads.

The leaves have a delicate flavour and a lettuce like texture. As a replacement for lettuce is their primary use in most recipes.

Beech

Fagus Sylvatica

Beech trees in the UK typically grow to heights of up to one hundred and twenty feet and have thick boles with pale grey bark. The leaves are small and oval in shape, being of a pale green colour. Beech leaves take longer than a year to decompose, creating a carpet of pale brown leaves beneath the tree year-round.

One of the largest broadleaf trees in the UK and easily recognisable, the beech tree used to be a favourite wood among furniture makers but now grows mainly on the edges of fields and in arboreta. Sometimes used as a hedging plant, this tree species is very slow growing but can reach impressive heights. The tallest native tree in the UK is a Beech, which has been measured at one hundred and forty-four feet tall.

The nuts or mast of this tree are produced in late summer, around September, and fall in large numbers. If you can beat the squirrels to collecting them, they can be eaten raw in small amounts, but are best roasted.

Each husk contains multiple nutlets which can be roasted like any nut and eaten.

Whilst I have some experience with this species, it is not one I turn to often as I find the husks difficult to get into for too small a reward due to the size of the nutlets.

Damsons

Prunus Domestica

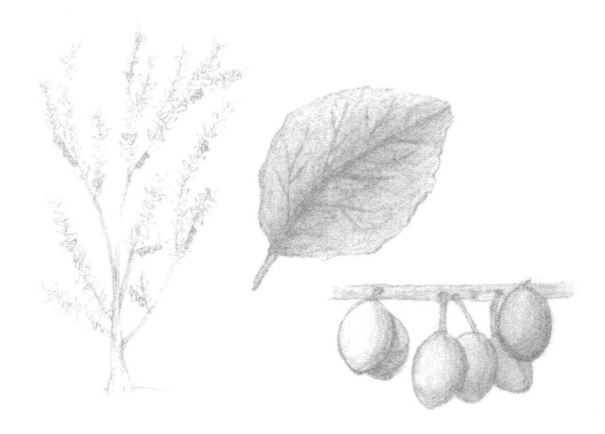

Damson trees grow to a typical height of around fifteen feet, with lance shaped leaves of dark green with a glossy coating. The fruit is a dark purple in colour.

Damsons, or wild plums, don't seem to me to be as common as they once were, but can still be found across the UK. Often seen in hedgerows, they are a beautiful wild food.

Damsons are one of the larger wild fruits of Britain, and whenever I happen to pass a fruiting damson tree on my travels, I always add a few fruits to my pack for later. The sugar boost is welcome on any hike, and they taste great.

Full of vitamin C, Damsons also contain sorbitol which can act as a laxative, so it's best not to eat too many when hiking to avoid too many toilet breaks.

Cat's Tails (Greater Reedmace)

Typha Latifolia

This species grows on the edge of lakes and ponds and reaches a height of around six feet. Characterised by the tall, thin stalks that support the seed heads and the long, thin leaves that grow closer to the base but reach almost to the top of the plant. The leaves look similar to grasses, but much larger. The edges of the leaves can be quite sharp.

Cat's tails, or greater reedmace, grows prolifically in waterways across Britain and is easily recognisable. In recent years, there have been numerous viral videos of American teenagers being told this plant is a wild corndog and having a horrible time eating the mature seed heads. I can't pretend that I did not pull similar pranks with the seed heads of this plant as a child.

In the context of wild food, the part of this plant that we are interested in is beneath the surface of the water. The root network of this plant is edible, and the rhizomes are a crunchy snack eaten raw, or a filling side when roasted in the ashes of your fire. The process of gathering them is often messy however, given that they grow on the edges of water ways wading through silt is a necessary evil to get at the edible parts of this species.

I haven't used this plant often, but in 2016 I walked from the south coast to the midlands and used this plant more than once during the journey.

Crab Apple

Malus sylvestris

Crab apple trees grow to a height of up to thirty feet and are irregular in shape.

Another staple of the English countryside, I come across less crab apple trees now than in years past, more often now I see cultivated apple trees growing at the side of roads due to people discarding apple cores from car windows. The only littering that I do not think entirely reprehensible.

True Crab Apples are much smaller and almost entirely unpalatable in their bitterness. Nevertheless, they are a favourite wild food of many people and indeed of mine, providing many impromptu lunches on the trail over the years. Once cooked, these fruits become much sweeter and can be made into sauces and pies that will be sure to impress your campmates and being naturally high in pectin, they are great for making jam.

Flowering in mid spring, the fruits are usually ready between late September and October, sometimes persisting on the tree until mid-winter, and have a multitude of uses in the kitchen as well as on the campfire.

The Bushcraft Camp

'Know, if though has a friend whom thou fully trustest, and from whom thou wouldst good derive, thou should blend thy mind with his, and gifts exchange, and often go to see him.'

Havamal: 44

The Bushcraft Camp

Saturday 8th April 2023

1500 hours

The Posset Cup – Portishead

This is the end of our trip; we are on our way home and have stopped at a Wetherspoons in Portishead. I have had no time at all for writing on this trip, so I have taken brief notes at rest points and am beginning to write them up now.

The beginning of our trip was typical of our lackadaisical style. We set off late with no real plan other than our starting point. Although on this occasion we had decided that we wouldn't hike too far and would focus more on bushcraft to hone our skills for the more serious trips this summer. Such as the lightweight trek along the southwest coast path planned for late May, we will likely have need of all our skills during this trip.

Our starting point was at the centre of the Forest of Dean.

When we left Chard this morning, we were sure that the Forest of Dean would be the perfect place to hole up for a few days without interruptions. Yet when we arrived at the densest, least populous area we could find on the map, it felt more like a Centreparcs than a wild place. Upon researching a little more, we discovered that wild camping was not well tolerated in this part of the forest and made the decision to move south-west into the Wye Valley.

We parked the pick-up truck in a remote-ish part of the valley and leaving our packs on the flatbed headed out to explore. I have kayaked and canoed long sections of the Wye, but had forgotten how lovely it was in springtime. Recent rain had the river in a fast-flowing half-flood. The water brown and churning from the runoff in the hills. It hadn't yet burst its banks, but the rapids at Symonds Yat were noisily beautiful. Along the banks the leaves on the beech trees were still in the almost translucent state of early springtime, casting a green haze over the forests.

We hiked to a pub called The Wye Not and discussed our plan for the evening. We were completely relaxed, despite the age of the day, and I felt we could easily have spent all evening by the fire in this little country pub. After all, when you have no destination, there's no rush to get there.

Examining our map, we noticed a small forest containing some caves only a short hike from where we had left the truck. Both of us having some fascination with geology, we decided that we would hike back up the hill and explore that area.

Finishing our drinks, the barkeep offered us some directions which we followed. We thanked him and began the walk. The hill felt a great deal steeper than it had any right to be, I was sure our hike down had held no real decline. But on this road, I was walking almost horizontally against the incline of the hill.

After some time, we came back upon the truck. The light was beginning to fade as late evening set in, so we claimed our packs from the flatbed and set out quickly.

Despite the considerable weight we were carrying (26kg each) this part of the days hiking was particularly enjoyable. The evening had cooled from the heat of the day and a light breeze blew through the valley. This forest had a carpet of wild garlic that lent it's pungence to the draft as we walked, and even my injured knee was behaving relatively well. Although our hike was short, and the distance small, given the late hour, darkness had fallen. The blackest of skies was peppered with silvering stars as we approached the mouth of the cave which we had come here to see.

Leaving our packs aground at the entrance, we lit up our torches and tentatively entered the cave. It was far larger than I had expected, although smaller than I had allowed myself to hope. A small family could live comfortably here I thought to myself. We later learned that they had, but that story comes later.

We explored every corner of this limestone nook as excited young boys adventuring through the fields of some far-off shire, and it was some time before we returned to the mouth where we had left our packs leaning against the stone. Rolling ourselves a cigarette and taking a drink, we discussed our next move. Both of us had become enamoured with this King Arthurs Cave, and we decided that we should like to pass the night inside.

Now, I understand that most people in this modern world would somewhat wilt at the very suggestion of bedding down in the cold damp dark of a limestone cave, but we are not most people, and it really was quite pleasant. A stiff wind had come up out of the south, while the cave was mostly dry and sheltered us. Pitching our hammocks between trees at the very mouth, we took the few steps into the second largest of the chambers and lit for ourselves a small fire in a crevice where it would leave no scarring, pouring ourselves each an ice-cold cider. I decided then that whilst the tranquillity was enjoyable, I would enjoy some music more deeply. I asked Will for his preference, and he suggested Heilung – Krigsgaldr, a fantastic choice. I played the entire album whilst we cooked and ate a simple meal. The album finished soon after the pots and pans had been cleaned, and I was lounged, chewing on dried beef. I found myself now in quite a bardic mood, meaning that I rather thought I would like some tales and some singing.

Taking our small lantern into the largest antechamber of the cave, I sang a slightly slower version of the first song to enter my mind. Helvegen by Wardruna. The cave rumbled the deeper notes and resonated the highest. I thoroughly enjoyed the experience of singing underground and found myself wishing that my wife Amelia was here to sing with me.

We returned to our small fire then and began looking up the cave's history. We discovered that this cave had in fact been inhabited, as we had suggested that it should have, for some thirty years by one Slippery Jem and his wife, Betsy. This piece of history was fascinating, but as interested as we were our conversation would likely make tiresome reading. So I'll not recount here the entirety of Slippery Jem's story, or of our conversations pertaining to him.

Instead, I will move onward to the details of our winding down.

Our evening of tales and song and cheer had left us happy and relaxed as we made our way to our hammocks at the cave's maw. Being so close as to be half inside the cave we had no need of our tarpaulins, so we left them packed. Preparing our sleeping bags we nibbled on travel rations, sipped ciders, and hummed along to the drums of Danheim. This good mood had to end eventually however, it was now approaching the middle night and we planned to arise an hour past the day side of the dawn. We settled into our hammocks and soon we were asleep.

The Bushcraft Camp

Sunday 9th April 2023

1900 hours

The Jackson House – Home Office

Once again, the location listed differs from the location described, but I had no more time in The Posset Cup and am continuing our story from the comfort of my chair by the fire.

To continue from where I left off, we awoke early the next morning. Perhaps ninety minutes post dawn, and despite being dampened by a predawn mist, we passed our first night as cave dwellers in comfort.

Having set no particular plans for the day ahead, we quickly enpacked our equipment and moved deeper into the cave to prepare a small breakfast and a cup of Yorkshire tea.

Over breakfast Will and I discussed what our next move should be. After some deliberation we decided that in the stead of staying sedentary and practicing some bushcraft skills as we had planned, that we would far rather explore the Wye valley of outstanding natural beauty in deeper detail. Whilst I had set myself for this trip to honing the skills that my hands were beginning to forget, such as bow drill, spindle, and ropemaking, I was more than happy to change tact and explore this beautiful landscape in the sunshine that we have so missed this past season.

Following our simple breakfast, we hiked back to the pickup truck at a leisurely pace. Stooping low to pick wild garlic, dandelion leaves, and cleavers as we walked. They should make a nice addition to the stew we planned on cooking tonight. The bags were slightly lighter this morning than they had been last night, but nevertheless my back was glad to be freed from the weight as we reached the truck.

Engorging ourselves on sunshine and springtime, we hiked packless through the valley of the wye until lunchtime, when the siren call of the pub became too much to resist. We sat ourselves down out of doors at a pub called the Saracens head, who served a fantastic, if not overly expensive, pint of Rhubarb Scrumpy. Will was particularly impressed by this, having never tried rhubarb ciders before, and proceeded to rave happily about it for a full five minutes in the warm and open manner that is typical of him when at ease.

Whilst Will utilised the facilities, I enjoyed my drink in the sunshine with the river Wye running noisily past us. I sat for some time just watching the ferryman take groups of walkers across the river, before I commenced a plan both secretive and days in the making.

Will's good friend Alfie had been intended to join us on this minor adventure from its inception, but was waylaid by business at home. Will's pet chicken Wallace was also intended to join us, but that's a story for a different volume. A few days before we were due to leave, Alfie's business cleared and he found himself suddenly available. Instead of coming with us openly, Alfie decided that he would track our location via my snapchat account and surprise us. A plan that he confided to my wife.

Knowing that I have a severe dislike of surprises, regardless of how pleasant they may be, my wife Amelia informed me of the plan so that I may prepare myself for it. We decided that Will should remain out of the loop however. With Alfie being his good friend and with Will not sharing my aversion to pleasant surprises, we felt that he would be happy to be joined unexpectedly. Here is detailed the complexities of this particular surprises' facilitation.

Alfie had left Chard early that morning, as farm business had kept him longer than expected the previous evening, and had driven directly for the Welsh border. But being a bank holiday weekend during the school's easter break, the traffic along the M5 had been horrendous. Alfie was a mere 14 miles away when I could no longer delay Will at the Saracens head. Leaving the Wye Valley by the northern road, Will and I returned to the A40 toward Monmouth. The lanes had been busy and had slowed us down enough that Alfie was waiting for us at a nearby service station.

Feigning a need for the facilities there I asked Will to pull over at that service station, a little over a mile ahead of us, but distracted by the music he missed the turning.

Alfie watched us go past and was ready to follow us at a reasonable distance to a town called Usk, where we pulled into a car park with toilets. To say that Will was surprised by Alfie's immediate arrival in the space next to us is an understatement. There was enough profanity that I imagine the more easily offended among my readership would be calling to ban this book were I to record it here verbatim.

Once the confusion was abated, and Alfie and I had explained our conspiracy to Will, we decided to give the vehicles a quick once over. Given the mileage done, and the age of Will's pickup truck, it is good practice. Now we turned our thoughts to a plan for the evening.

Spreading the maps out on the bonnet of Alfie's Mitsubishi L200 we discovered a lake not too far away. Given its large size and proximity to civilisation we knew that it was extremely unlikely to contain a suitable location for us to wild camp in, but as a group we decided to scout it out nonetheless. Time enjoyed can never be time wasted.

Will and I followed behind Alfie's much larger vehicle along the lanes to our location and pulled into the car park of a golf club that was to give us our first views of the lake. Our map had given us the impression that access to the lake would be available here, but the map's impressions were misleading. It took less than ten minutes for us to realise that to access this body of water we would have to re-enter our vehicles and approach from another direction. Our next angle of approach led us to the very edge of the water, and a large, heavily populated boating club.

Whilst of course, this was no good for wild camping, it gave us a view of a beautiful area. Having spent much of my formative years among vessels of varying kind, I enjoyed being afforded a window-view into that world by the sight of kayaks, canoes and small sailing vessels drifting lazily in the sunshine across the surface of the water.

We proceeded to hike around the perimeter of the lake for the next two and a half hours. Half in the hope of finding an appropriate stealth camping spot, and half just for the joy of hiking by a lake in the March sunshine.

It should go without saying that although we found no suitably stealthy location, we thoroughly enjoyed the exploration. Of course, if we had succeeded in finding somewhere suitable, we would have been trespassing and I would have been unable to detail it here.

Eventually, we headed back to the trucks, and decided the best course of action would be to head back to the cave of Mr Slippery Jem.

The Cave – Night Two

The route back to the cave was uneventful. We walked slowly and abreast across the garlic carpeted forest until the cave came suddenly into our line of sight. Deciding against spending another night underground to avoid repetition, we lay our packs aground in the same location as we had the night before and began a reconnaissance expedition to find a suitable place to set up for the night.

It was Alfie that chose our location, and he chose well. Isolated, densely forested, and close to a cliff edge, this location gave us a clear view of the night sky without exposing us to the elements. It was the perfect location for camping in spring.

As it was still only mid-afternoon, we had plenty of time, and plenty of light, to explore by. We soon discovered that this location had been used before, and in the relatively recent past. Most likely during the final weeks of the previous summer. We quickly uncovered a small firepit which had been hidden beneath the autumnal detritus of the towering beech trees surrounding us.

A short distance away we found some cut rounds of oak, perfect for use as camp chairs, and we discovered and collected multiple discarded items of camping paraphernalia. This overgrown camp was likely the result of young people packing up their equipment whilst hung over and accidentally leaving things behind. I suppose most of us were guilty of this in our younger days at some point or another.

After a very brief respite to stretch our muscles and catch our breath from the short but steep hike from the cave to the location of tonight's refuge, preparations began.

Not a single word was spoken. Alfie began collecting and assembling brash for his natural shelter. Will gathered firewood and I assembled both my hammock, and Will's. I was struck by the efficiency of the process, and by how effectively we each set ourselves to our individual tasks with zero verbal communication. It was nice to be working with others as experienced and professional as myself.

Within a very short time, camp was fully assembled, everyone had a bed, and our equipment was organised carefully. We reclined ourselves around the empty firepit, smoking leisurely and sipping on ciders to an old Waylon Jennings country song, played on a small Bluetooth speaker that Alfie had had the foresight to bring along.

Whilst we had not done anything particularly bushcraft-y on our adventure so far, (save Alfie's natural shelter, of which I will talk more later), we had a few hours left before sundown to get a little of that sort of thing done. None of us were particularly in the mood or mindset for demonstrating any of the more labour-intensive skills, however. Such skills as bow drill or wood carving. Leaving us to mostly discuss theory.

We began by discussing various knots and their merits, starting off with the truckers hitch before moving on to the clove hitch, the bowline, and various slipknots. Very quickly it became obvious that whilst all of us have some basic skills in this area, none of us use any of these knots with any real frequency, with the possible exception of the trucker's hitch. We wondered at this for a while before moving on.

For a long while now, we discussed indigenous tree species. A subject that I have been known to have a passion for that borders on the obsessive and have often been accused of being supremely boring when talking about trees at any length. Luckily, I was with two other such enthusiasts and there was no danger of my expertise being deemed in any way dull. Being in a broadleaf forest we mostly discussed species like Beech, Holly, Oak, and Birch. This led Alfie to share some of his considerable knowledge of indigenous mycology, a subject that Will and I were both greatly appreciative of being educated in. Although I will stick to my word and exclude any talk of mushrooms as food, I will say that we spent a long time discussing the varying suspected medicinal applications of the species named as Trametes Versicolor.

By now we had spoken for such a time that the day had grown long. The light was beginning to fail. It was time to light a fire.

Alfie again took the lead here. While we all have considerable expertise in this area, it worked out well as he used methods that I have never before seen used successfully.

Alfie piled finger sized beech sticks in a Jenga like fashion, leaving open a space in the centre. Placing thin birch twigs and dry beech leaves into the opening, he proceeded to use his knife to shave a large amount of magnesium into the centre from a rod that had been secured inside his tinder box.

Now, I have seen magnesium used as an accelerant in this context, but never counted it to be worth the effort. That's not what Alfie was doing. In Alfie's method the magnesium itself was the tinder to be used to produce the first flame. I'll admit that I entirely anticipated failure for this method. I should have more faith in his skills in future, because it worked. He showered the magnesium filings with a heavy dousing of bright sparks from his ferrocerium rod and to my amazement and contradiction, the filings came quickly to a bright white flame, igniting his kindling with ease. I felt no shame in admitting that I was impressed by this display of new methods. I suppose it is true then, that man is forever a student.

Within minutes the small fire was stable. And being comprised mostly of well-seasoned beech burned in the round, was beginning to sustain a large and efficient base of embers. The air flow in this campsite was perfect, a stiff breeze flowed across the ground from the cliff side to the south of us, fanning our flames and blowing what little smoke was produced cleanly away to be dissipated by the wood of the forest.

Next came the time for cooking. We hadn't eaten a particularly great deal during the day and were all looking forward to a hot meal by the fire.

For this purpose, I had carried with me some vegetables. I had brought potatoes, carrots, radishes, an onion, and a cabbage, along with some chicken stock cubes. I intended to recreate a thinner incarnation of a winter favourite of my house. A recipe I call dozen broth. A simple vegetable stew, properly seasoned with coarse sea salt, coarse ground black pepper, and extra hot chilli powder. Unfortunately, I couldn't reasonably carry the dozen different vegetables that the original recipe requires, so this would be a poor imitation and far less hearty. But worse than that, almost incomprehensibly worse, I had forgotten to pack the spices. I found myself thinking of the character Samwise Gamgee in Tolkien's Lord of The Rings, carrying seasonings to the edge of the world so as never to have to serve food unseasoned, and reprimanded myself for being so forgetful. Nevertheless, we had to make do, and between Will and I we managed to produce a stew that was more than just edible. Adding the generous bundle of wild garlic, dandelion leaf, and wild cleavers that we had foraged the previous day gave a springtime essence to our meal that was both nutritious and heartening. We ate in near silence to the music of Tyler Childers and relaxed by the fire, each nursing a cold cider. Being still, and so close to perfect quiet, we saw a small herd of fallow dear pass us by within a distance of perhaps only one hundred feet.

A sure sign that we were well camouflaged from the rest of the forest.

Of course, three young men, in good company and in good spirits, could no more easily spend all night discussing business than anyone else, and so conversation inevitably turned over to more interesting topics. We discussed current events, world politics, relationships, and Will's most current romantic endeavours. I doubt that the inappropriate nature of this conversation for print needs to be stated here.

The night was long and the full moon high by the time I felt the need to retire. As the oldest of the group, and in the worst health, I was usually inclined to retire earlier than they. I climbed into my hammock gratefully, thankful for the support for a weary back, and attempted to continue the conversation from a position of comfort. The music changed from country ballads to Chopin. Nocturnes, op 9:1. Larghetto played skilfully by Brigitte Engerer being a particularly clear remembrance for me. Of course, with a clear sky of shimmering stars above me, the moon casting deep shadows about me and the silhouettes of two men that I trusted flickering companionably in the firelight in front of me, I fell easily into a peaceful and dreamless slumber that carried me cleanly into tomorrow's frosty dawn.

The Final Day

Despite the others being to bed much later than myself, they awoke and arose far earlier, and as such there was a small fire burning, with tea brewing, by the time I left the comforting sanctuary of my hammock. As much as I enjoy the challenge of experiencing the outdoors alone, there is something particularly special about waking to cold dawn air, the smell of wood smoke and the whistling sounds of a camp kettle accompanied by friendly voices softly raised.

Despite the lazy start, we wasted little time in disassembling our little camp. With less time than I would have liked to acclimatise to the cold of dawn, we ate a hasty breakfast of oats and packed our equipment. We had created rather more waste than I expected, and we spent a short time diligently gathering it all into what Will colloquially refers to as a 'Gash Bag'. Ensuring that there was no trace of our passing is as natural to each of us as breathing.

We packed away our camp in the same companionable silence in which it had been constructed. Once again, I was stricken with pride to be accompanied by such competent men.

There is little more to be said of the events of this last day. We all had things to be getting back to. I, my wife and child. Alfie his farm. Will his romantic endeavours and his curious pet chicken. As melancholy as the last day of any adventure surely must be, I took heart at the prospect of being reunited with my family. Despite being away for a mere three days, I had missed them.

Shouldering our packs, we began the short hike back to the trucks. We arrived in less than an hour despite the sharp incline. Unburdening ourselves directly into the flatbeds of the trucks, we immediately began discussing our next course of action. Alfie's farm business called him to return home promptly, but Will and I preferred a slower route in more northern fashion.

Of course, that means in simple terms that we would take a more circuitous route so as to include a pub.

This led us nicely to The Posset Cup in Portishead where this writing began. A circuitous literary route for a rather circuitous journey. How apropos.

Northernism, don't exclude it.

Alfie's Shelter

At the beginning of writing 'The Bushcraft Camp', I had fully intended on including a visual representation of the shelter that Alfie built for himself that last night. But it surpasses my skill in artistry to do so, and the illustrator of the rest of the book is kept busy with other projects. Instead, I will attempt to describe it as best I can after my own fashion.

Choosing two young beech trees on the north western side of our camp, Alfie set about finding suitable dead limbs to create 'A' frames on the outer side of each bole. These 'A' frames were lashed with a small amount of jute fibre at the height of a man's shoulder, and kept to a steep angling of around 35 degrees.

Atop those 'A' shaped framings Alfie lay another, longer beech branch. Bringing the width of his construction to a little over five and a half feet.

To prevent the wind from creating a chill, he then hammered four stakes into the soft earth between the two trees and constructed a wall of logs and debris to around three feet high. Leaving himself a window between wall and roof to allow for ventilation and the letting in of moonlight.

Pruning the still green branches of a wind-fallen Balsam Fir, Alfie then built for himself a fragrant bed of needles, and using further branches, constructed walls of green at each triangular side of his shelter.

With three walls of his endeavour completed, Alfie then lashed his small tarpaulin onto the front of his shelter at three corners. Choosing to toggle one corner upward for an entrance that can be sealed against the rain at need.

Now completed, it was mentioned that were we here to hunt, his small shelter constituted a near perfect hunters hide.

Stretching out his thick sleeping pad and thin sleeping bag, Alfie looked to be very comfortable as he tested his beds suitability.

Printed in Great Britain
by Amazon